C-2280 CAREER EXAMINATION SERIES

This is your
PASSBOOK for...

Mail Clerk

Test Preparation Study Guide
Questions & Answers

COPYRIGHT NOTICE

This book is SOLELY intended for, is sold ONLY to, and its use is RESTRICTED to individual, bona fide applicants or candidates who qualify by virtue of having seriously filed applications for appropriate license, certificate, professional and/or promotional advancement, higher school matriculation, scholarship, or other legitimate requirements of education and/or governmental authorities.

This book is NOT intended for use, class instruction, tutoring, training, duplication, copying, reprinting, excerption, or adaptation, etc., by:

1) Other publishers
2) Proprietors and/or Instructors of "Coaching" and/or Preparatory Courses
3) Personnel and/or Training Divisions of commercial, industrial, and governmental organizations
4) Schools, colleges, or universities and/or their departments and staffs, including teachers and other personnel
5) Testing Agencies or Bureaus
6) Study groups which seek by the purchase of a single volume to copy and/or duplicate and/or adapt this material for use by the group as a whole without having purchased individual volumes for each of the members of the group
7) Et al.

Such persons would be in violation of appropriate Federal and State statutes.

PROVISION OF LICENSING AGREEMENTS – Recognized educational, commercial, industrial, and governmental institutions and organizations, and others legitimately engaged in educational pursuits, including training, testing, and measurement activities, may address request for a licensing agreement to the copyright owners, who will determine whether, and under what conditions, including fees and charges, the materials in this book may be used them. In other words, a licensing facility exists for the legitimate use of the material in this book on other than an individual basis. However, it is asseverated and affirmed here that the material in this book CANNOT be used without the receipt of the express permission of such a licensing agreement from the Publishers. Inquiries re licensing should be addressed to the company, attention rights and permissions department.

All rights reserved, including the right of reproduction in whole or in part, in any form or by any means, electronic or mechanical, including photocopying, recording, or by any information storage and retrieval system, without permission in writing from the Publisher.

Copyright © 2024 by
National Learning Corporation

212 Michael Drive, Syosset, NY 11791
(516) 921-8888 • www.passbooks.com
E-mail: info@passbooks.com

PUBLISHED IN THE UNITED STATES OF AMERICA

PASSBOOK® SERIES

THE *PASSBOOK® SERIES* has been created to prepare applicants and candidates for the ultimate academic battlefield – the examination room.

At some time in our lives, each and every one of us may be required to take an examination – for validation, matriculation, admission, qualification, registration, certification, or licensure.

Based on the assumption that every applicant or candidate has met the basic formal educational standards, has taken the required number of courses, and read the necessary texts, the *PASSBOOK® SERIES* furnishes the one special preparation which may assure passing with confidence, instead of failing with insecurity. Examination questions – together with answers – are furnished as the basic vehicle for study so that the mysteries of the examination and its compounding difficulties may be eliminated or diminished by a sure method.

This book is meant to help you pass your examination provided that you qualify and are serious in your objective.

The entire field is reviewed through the huge store of content information which is succinctly presented through a provocative and challenging approach – the question-and-answer method.

A climate of success is established by furnishing the correct answers at the end of each test.

You soon learn to recognize types of questions, forms of questions, and patterns of questioning. You may even begin to anticipate expected outcomes.

You perceive that many questions are repeated or adapted so that you can gain acute insights, which may enable you to score many sure points.

You learn how to confront new questions, or types of questions, and to attack them confidently and work out the correct answers.

You note objectives and emphases, and recognize pitfalls and dangers, so that you may make positive educational adjustments.

Moreover, you are kept fully informed in relation to new concepts, methods, practices, and directions in the field.

You discover that you are actually taking the examination all the time: you are preparing for the examination by "taking" an examination, not by reading extraneous and/or supererogatory textbooks.

In short, this PASSBOOK®, used directedly, should be an important factor in helping you to pass your test.

MAIL CLERK

DUTIES
This is routine clerical and manual work involving the receiving, sorting and routing of both incoming and outgoing mail and the receiving and distribution of ordered items. An employee in this class performs the duties connected with mail distribution in a public jurisdiction. The job involves sorting and delivering of mail and internal communications. The incumbent may be assigned to clerical tasks when not needed for mail work. Does related work as required.

SCOPE OF THE EXAMINATION
The <u>written test</u> will cover knowledge, skills and/or abilities in such areas as:

1. Clerical abilities;
2. Filing;
3. Understanding and interpreting written material;
4. Organizing data into tables;
5. Proofreading; and
6. Map reading.

HOW TO TAKE A TEST

I. YOU MUST PASS AN EXAMINATION

A. *WHAT EVERY CANDIDATE SHOULD KNOW*

Examination applicants often ask us for help in preparing for the written test. What can I study in advance? What kinds of questions will be asked? How will the test be given? How will the papers be graded?

As an applicant for a civil service examination, you may be wondering about some of these things. Our purpose here is to suggest effective methods of advance study and to describe civil service examinations.

Your chances for success on this examination can be increased if you know how to prepare. Those "pre-examination jitters" can be reduced if you know what to expect. You can even experience an adventure in good citizenship if you know why civil service exams are given.

B. *WHY ARE CIVIL SERVICE EXAMINATIONS GIVEN?*

Civil service examinations are important to you in two ways. As a citizen, you want public jobs filled by employees who know how to do their work. As a job seeker, you want a fair chance to compete for that job on an equal footing with other candidates. The best-known means of accomplishing this two-fold goal is the competitive examination.

Exams are widely publicized throughout the nation. They may be administered for jobs in federal, state, city, municipal, town or village governments or agencies.

Any citizen may apply, with some limitations, such as the age or residence of applicants. Your experience and education may be reviewed to see whether you meet the requirements for the particular examination. When these requirements exist, they are reasonable and applied consistently to all applicants. Thus, a competitive examination may cause you some uneasiness now, but it is your privilege and safeguard.

C. *HOW ARE CIVIL SERVICE EXAMS DEVELOPED?*

Examinations are carefully written by trained technicians who are specialists in the field known as "psychological measurement," in consultation with recognized authorities in the field of work that the test will cover. These experts recommend the subject matter areas or skills to be tested; only those knowledges or skills important to your success on the job are included. The most reliable books and source materials available are used as references. Together, the experts and technicians judge the difficulty level of the questions.

Test technicians know how to phrase questions so that the problem is clearly stated. Their ethics do not permit "trick" or "catch" questions. Questions may have been tried out on sample groups, or subjected to statistical analysis, to determine their usefulness.

Written tests are often used in combination with performance tests, ratings of training and experience, and oral interviews. All of these measures combine to form the best-known means of finding the right person for the right job.

II. HOW TO PASS THE WRITTEN TEST

A. NATURE OF THE EXAMINATION

To prepare intelligently for civil service examinations, you should know how they differ from school examinations you have taken. In school you were assigned certain definite pages to read or subjects to cover. The examination questions were quite detailed and usually emphasized memory. Civil service exams, on the other hand, try to discover your present ability to perform the duties of a position, plus your potentiality to learn these duties. In other words, a civil service exam attempts to predict how successful you will be. Questions cover such a broad area that they cannot be as minute and detailed as school exam questions.

In the public service similar kinds of work, or positions, are grouped together in one "class." This process is known as *position-classification*. All the positions in a class are paid according to the salary range for that class. One class title covers all of these positions, and they are all tested by the same examination.

B. FOUR BASIC STEPS

1) Study the announcement

How, then, can you know what subjects to study? Our best answer is: "Learn as much as possible about the class of positions for which you've applied." The exam will test the knowledge, skills and abilities needed to do the work.

Your most valuable source of information about the position you want is the official exam announcement. This announcement lists the training and experience qualifications. Check these standards and apply only if you come reasonably close to meeting them.

The brief description of the position in the examination announcement offers some clues to the subjects which will be tested. Think about the job itself. Review the duties in your mind. Can you perform them, or are there some in which you are rusty? Fill in the blank spots in your preparation.

Many jurisdictions preview the written test in the exam announcement by including a section called "Knowledge and Abilities Required," "Scope of the Examination," or some similar heading. Here you will find out specifically what fields will be tested.

2) Review your own background

Once you learn in general what the position is all about, and what you need to know to do the work, ask yourself which subjects you already know fairly well and which need improvement. You may wonder whether to concentrate on improving your strong areas or on building some background in your fields of weakness. When the announcement has specified "some knowledge" or "considerable knowledge," or has used adjectives like "beginning principles of..." or "advanced ... methods," you can get a clue as to the number and difficulty of questions to be asked in any given field. More questions, and hence broader coverage, would be included for those subjects which are more important in the work. Now weigh your strengths and weaknesses against the job requirements and prepare accordingly.

3) Determine the level of the position

Another way to tell how intensively you should prepare is to understand the level of the job for which you are applying. Is it the entering level? In other words, is this the position in which beginners in a field of work are hired? Or is it an intermediate or advanced level? Sometimes this is indicated by such words as "Junior" or "Senior" in the class title. Other jurisdictions use Roman numerals to designate the level – Clerk I, Clerk II, for example. The word "Supervisor" sometimes appears in the title. If the level is not indicated by the title, check the description of duties. Will you be working under very close supervision, or will you have responsibility for independent decisions in this work?

4) Choose appropriate study materials

Now that you know the subjects to be examined and the relative amount of each subject to be covered, you can choose suitable study materials. For beginning level jobs, or even advanced ones, if you have a pronounced weakness in some aspect of your training, read a modern, standard textbook in that field. Be sure it is up to date and has general coverage. Such books are normally available at your library, and the librarian will be glad to help you locate one. For entry-level positions, questions of appropriate difficulty are chosen -- neither highly advanced questions, nor those too simple. Such questions require careful thought but not advanced training.

If the position for which you are applying is technical or advanced, you will read more advanced, specialized material. If you are already familiar with the basic principles of your field, elementary textbooks would waste your time. Concentrate on advanced textbooks and technical periodicals. Think through the concepts and review difficult problems in your field.

These are all general sources. You can get more ideas on your own initiative, following these leads. For example, training manuals and publications of the government agency which employs workers in your field can be useful, particularly for technical and professional positions. A letter or visit to the government department involved may result in more specific study suggestions, and certainly will provide you with a more definite idea of the exact nature of the position you are seeking.

III. KINDS OF TESTS

Tests are used for purposes other than measuring knowledge and ability to perform specified duties. For some positions, it is equally important to test ability to make adjustments to new situations or to profit from training. In others, basic mental abilities not dependent on information are essential. Questions which test these things may not appear as pertinent to the duties of the position as those which test for knowledge and information. Yet they are often highly important parts of a fair examination. For very general questions, it is almost impossible to help you direct your study efforts. What we can do is to point out some of the more common of these general abilities needed in public service positions and describe some typical questions.

1) General information

Broad, general information has been found useful for predicting job success in some kinds of work. This is tested in a variety of ways, from vocabulary lists to questions about current events. Basic background in some field of work, such as sociology or economics, may be sampled in a group of questions. Often these are principles which have become familiar to most persons through exposure rather than through formal training. It is difficult to advise you how to study for these questions; being alert to the world around you is our best suggestion.

2) Verbal ability

An example of an ability needed in many positions is verbal or language ability. Verbal ability is, in brief, the ability to use and understand words. Vocabulary and grammar tests are typical measures of this ability. Reading comprehension or paragraph interpretation questions are common in many kinds of civil service tests. You are given a paragraph of written material and asked to find its central meaning.

3) Numerical ability

Number skills can be tested by the familiar arithmetic problem, by checking paired lists of numbers to see which are alike and which are different, or by interpreting charts and graphs. In the latter test, a graph may be printed in the test booklet which you are asked to use as the basis for answering questions.

4) Observation

A popular test for law-enforcement positions is the observation test. A picture is shown to you for several minutes, then taken away. Questions about the picture test your ability to observe both details and larger elements.

5) Following directions

In many positions in the public service, the employee must be able to carry out written instructions dependably and accurately. You may be given a chart with several columns, each column listing a variety of information. The questions require you to carry out directions involving the information given in the chart.

6) Skills and aptitudes

Performance tests effectively measure some manual skills and aptitudes. When the skill is one in which you are trained, such as typing or shorthand, you can practice. These tests are often very much like those given in business school or high school courses. For many of the other skills and aptitudes, however, no short-time preparation can be made. Skills and abilities natural to you or that you have developed throughout your lifetime are being tested.

Many of the general questions just described provide all the data needed to answer the questions and ask you to use your reasoning ability to find the answers. Your best preparation for these tests, as well as for tests of facts and ideas, is to be at your physical and mental best. You, no doubt, have your own methods of getting into an exam-taking mood and keeping "in shape." The next section lists some ideas on this subject.

IV. KINDS OF QUESTIONS

Only rarely is the "essay" question, which you answer in narrative form, used in civil service tests. Civil service tests are usually of the short-answer type. Full instructions for answering these questions will be given to you at the examination. But in case this is your first experience with short-answer questions and separate answer sheets, here is what you need to know:

1) Multiple-choice Questions

Most popular of the short-answer questions is the "multiple choice" or "best answer" question. It can be used, for example, to test for factual knowledge, ability to solve problems or judgment in meeting situations found at work.

A multiple-choice question is normally one of three types—
- It can begin with an incomplete statement followed by several possible endings. You are to find the one ending which *best* completes the statement, although some of the others may not be entirely wrong.
- It can also be a complete statement in the form of a question which is answered by choosing one of the statements listed.

- It can be in the form of a problem – again you select the best answer.

Here is an example of a multiple-choice question with a discussion which should give you some clues as to the method for choosing the right answer:

When an employee has a complaint about his assignment, the action which will *best* help him overcome his difficulty is to
- A. discuss his difficulty with his coworkers
- B. take the problem to the head of the organization
- C. take the problem to the person who gave him the assignment
- D. say nothing to anyone about his complaint

In answering this question, you should study each of the choices to find which is best. Consider choice "A" – Certainly an employee may discuss his complaint with fellow employees, but no change or improvement can result, and the complaint remains unresolved. Choice "B" is a poor choice since the head of the organization probably does not know what assignment you have been given, and taking your problem to him is known as "going over the head" of the supervisor. The supervisor, or person who made the assignment, is the person who can clarify it or correct any injustice. Choice "C" is, therefore, correct. To say nothing, as in choice "D," is unwise. Supervisors have and interest in knowing the problems employees are facing, and the employee is seeking a solution to his problem.

2) True/False Questions

The "true/false" or "right/wrong" form of question is sometimes used. Here a complete statement is given. Your job is to decide whether the statement is right or wrong.

SAMPLE: A roaming cell-phone call to a nearby city costs less than a non-roaming call to a distant city.

This statement is wrong, or false, since roaming calls are more expensive.

This is not a complete list of all possible question forms, although most of the others are variations of these common types. You will always get complete directions for answering questions. Be sure you understand *how* to mark your answers – ask questions until you do.

V. RECORDING YOUR ANSWERS

Computer terminals are used more and more today for many different kinds of exams.

For an examination with very few applicants, you may be told to record your answers in the test booklet itself. Separate answer sheets are much more common. If this separate answer sheet is to be scored by machine – and this is often the case – it is highly important that you mark your answers correctly in order to get credit.

An electronic scoring machine is often used in civil service offices because of the speed with which papers can be scored. Machine-scored answer sheets must be marked with a pencil, which will be given to you. This pencil has a high graphite content which responds to the electronic scoring machine. As a matter of fact, stray dots may register as answers, so do not let your pencil rest on the answer sheet while you are pondering the correct answer. Also, if your pencil lead breaks or is otherwise defective, ask for another.

Since the answer sheet will be dropped in a slot in the scoring machine, be careful not to bend the corners or get the paper crumpled.

The answer sheet normally has five vertical columns of numbers, with 30 numbers to a column. These numbers correspond to the question numbers in your test booklet. After each number, going across the page are four or five pairs of dotted lines. These short dotted lines have small letters or numbers above them. The first two pairs may also have a "T" or "F" above the letters. This indicates that the first two pairs only are to be used if the questions are of the true-false type. If the questions are multiple choice, disregard the "T" and "F" and pay attention only to the small letters or numbers.

Answer your questions in the manner of the sample that follows:

32. The largest city in the United States is
    A. Washington, D.C.
    B. New York City
    C. Chicago
    D. Detroit
    E. San Francisco

1) Choose the answer you think is best. (New York City is the largest, so "B" is correct.)
2) Find the row of dotted lines numbered the same as the question you are answering. (Find row number 32)
3) Find the pair of dotted lines corresponding to the answer. (Find the pair of lines under the mark "B.")
4) Make a solid black mark between the dotted lines.

VI. BEFORE THE TEST

Common sense will help you find procedures to follow to get ready for an examination. Too many of us, however, overlook these sensible measures. Indeed, nervousness and fatigue have been found to be the most serious reasons why applicants fail to do their best on civil service tests. Here is a list of reminders:

- Begin your preparation early – Don't wait until the last minute to go scurrying around for books and materials or to find out what the position is all about.
- Prepare continuously – An hour a night for a week is better than an all-night cram session. This has been definitely established. What is more, a night a week for a month will return better dividends than crowding your study into a shorter period of time.
- Locate the place of the exam – You have been sent a notice telling you when and where to report for the examination. If the location is in a different town or otherwise unfamiliar to you, it would be well to inquire the best route and learn something about the building.
- Relax the night before the test – Allow your mind to rest. Do not study at all that night. Plan some mild recreation or diversion; then go to bed early and get a good night's sleep.
- Get up early enough to make a leisurely trip to the place for the test – This way unforeseen events, traffic snarls, unfamiliar buildings, etc. will not upset you.
- Dress comfortably – A written test is not a fashion show. You will be known by number and not by name, so wear something comfortable.

- Leave excess paraphernalia at home – Shopping bags and odd bundles will get in your way. You need bring only the items mentioned in the official notice you received; usually everything you need is provided. Do not bring reference books to the exam. They will only confuse those last minutes and be taken away from you when in the test room.
- Arrive somewhat ahead of time – If because of transportation schedules you must get there very early, bring a newspaper or magazine to take your mind off yourself while waiting.
- Locate the examination room – When you have found the proper room, you will be directed to the seat or part of the room where you will sit. Sometimes you are given a sheet of instructions to read while you are waiting. Do not fill out any forms until you are told to do so; just read them and be prepared.
- Relax and prepare to listen to the instructions
- If you have any physical problem that may keep you from doing your best, be sure to tell the test administrator. If you are sick or in poor health, you really cannot do your best on the exam. You can come back and take the test some other time.

VII. AT THE TEST

The day of the test is here and you have the test booklet in your hand. The temptation to get going is very strong. Caution! There is more to success than knowing the right answers. You must know how to identify your papers and understand variations in the type of short-answer question used in this particular examination. Follow these suggestions for maximum results from your efforts:

1) Cooperate with the monitor

The test administrator has a duty to create a situation in which you can be as much at ease as possible. He will give instructions, tell you when to begin, check to see that you are marking your answer sheet correctly, and so on. He is not there to guard you, although he will see that your competitors do not take unfair advantage. He wants to help you do your best.

2) Listen to all instructions

Don't jump the gun! Wait until you understand all directions. In most civil service tests you get more time than you need to answer the questions. So don't be in a hurry. Read each word of instructions until you clearly understand the meaning. Study the examples, listen to all announcements and follow directions. Ask questions if you do not understand what to do.

3) Identify your papers

Civil service exams are usually identified by number only. You will be assigned a number; you must not put your name on your test papers. Be sure to copy your number correctly. Since more than one exam may be given, copy your exact examination title.

4) Plan your time

Unless you are told that a test is a "speed" or "rate of work" test, speed itself is usually not important. Time enough to answer all the questions will be provided, but this does not mean that you have all day. An overall time limit has been set. Divide the total time (in minutes) by the number of questions to determine the approximate time you have for each question.

5) Do not linger over difficult questions

If you come across a difficult question, mark it with a paper clip (useful to have along) and come back to it when you have been through the booklet. One caution if you do this – be sure to skip a number on your answer sheet as well. Check often to be sure that you have not lost your place and that you are marking in the row numbered the same as the question you are answering.

6) Read the questions

Be sure you know what the question asks! Many capable people are unsuccessful because they failed to *read* the questions correctly.

7) Answer all questions

Unless you have been instructed that a penalty will be deducted for incorrect answers, it is better to guess than to omit a question.

8) Speed tests

It is often better NOT to guess on speed tests. It has been found that on timed tests people are tempted to spend the last few seconds before time is called in marking answers at random – without even reading them – in the hope of picking up a few extra points. To discourage this practice, the instructions may warn you that your score will be "corrected" for guessing. That is, a penalty will be applied. The incorrect answers will be deducted from the correct ones, or some other penalty formula will be used.

9) Review your answers

If you finish before time is called, go back to the questions you guessed or omitted to give them further thought. Review other answers if you have time.

10) Return your test materials

If you are ready to leave before others have finished or time is called, take ALL your materials to the monitor and leave quietly. Never take any test material with you. The monitor can discover whose papers are not complete, and taking a test booklet may be grounds for disqualification.

VIII. EXAMINATION TECHNIQUES

1) Read the general instructions carefully. These are usually printed on the first page of the exam booklet. As a rule, these instructions refer to the timing of the examination; the fact that you should not start work until the signal and must stop work at a signal, etc. If there are any *special* instructions, such as a choice of questions to be answered, make sure that you note this instruction carefully.

2) When you are ready to start work on the examination, that is as soon as the signal has been given, read the instructions to each question booklet, underline any key words or phrases, such as *least, best, outline, describe* and the like. In this way you will tend to answer as requested rather than discover on reviewing your paper that you *listed without describing*, that you selected the *worst* choice rather than the *best* choice, etc.

3) If the examination is of the objective or multiple-choice type – that is, each question will also give a series of possible answers: A, B, C or D, and you are called upon to select the best answer and write the letter next to that answer on your answer paper – it is advisable to start answering each question in turn. There may be anywhere from 50 to 100 such questions in the three or four hours allotted and you can see how much time would be taken if you read through all the questions before beginning to answer any. Furthermore, if you come across a question or group of questions which you know would be difficult to answer, it would undoubtedly affect your handling of all the other questions.

4) If the examination is of the essay type and contains but a few questions, it is a moot point as to whether you should read all the questions before starting to answer any one. Of course, if you are given a choice – say five out of seven and the like – then it is essential to read all the questions so you can eliminate the two that are most difficult. If, however, you are asked to answer all the questions, there may be danger in trying to answer the easiest one first because you may find that you will spend too much time on it. The best technique is to answer the first question, then proceed to the second, etc.

5) Time your answers. Before the exam begins, write down the time it started, then add the time allowed for the examination and write down the time it must be completed, then divide the time available somewhat as follows:
    - If 3-1/2 hours are allowed, that would be 210 minutes. If you have 80 objective-type questions, that would be an average of 2-1/2 minutes per question. Allow yourself no more than 2 minutes per question, or a total of 160 minutes, which will permit about 50 minutes to review.
    - If for the time allotment of 210 minutes there are 7 essay questions to answer, that would average about 30 minutes a question. Give yourself only 25 minutes per question so that you have about 35 minutes to review.

6) The most important instruction is to *read each question* and make sure you know what is wanted. The second most important instruction is to *time yourself properly* so that you answer every question. The third most important instruction is to *answer every question*. Guess if you have to but include something for each question. Remember that you will receive no credit for a blank and will probably receive some credit if you write something in answer to an essay question. If you guess a letter – say "B" for a multiple-choice question – you may have guessed right. If you leave a blank as an answer to a multiple-choice question, the examiners may respect your feelings but it will not add a point to your score. Some exams may penalize you for wrong answers, so in such cases *only*, you may not want to guess unless you have some basis for your answer.

7) Suggestions
    a. Objective-type questions
        1. Examine the question booklet for proper sequence of pages and questions
        2. Read all instructions carefully
        3. Skip any question which seems too difficult; return to it after all other questions have been answered
        4. Apportion your time properly; do not spend too much time on any single question or group of questions

5. Note and underline key words – *all, most, fewest, least, best, worst, same, opposite,* etc.
6. Pay particular attention to negatives
7. Note unusual option, e.g., unduly long, short, complex, different or similar in content to the body of the question
8. Observe the use of "hedging" words – *probably, may, most likely,* etc.
9. Make sure that your answer is put next to the same number as the question
10. Do not second-guess unless you have good reason to believe the second answer is definitely more correct
11. Cross out original answer if you decide another answer is more accurate; do not erase until you are ready to hand your paper in
12. Answer all questions; guess unless instructed otherwise
13. Leave time for review

b. Essay questions
   1. Read each question carefully
   2. Determine exactly what is wanted. Underline key words or phrases.
   3. Decide on outline or paragraph answer
   4. Include many different points and elements unless asked to develop any one or two points or elements
   5. Show impartiality by giving pros and cons unless directed to select one side only
   6. Make and write down any assumptions you find necessary to answer the questions
   7. Watch your English, grammar, punctuation and choice of words
   8. Time your answers; don't crowd material

8) Answering the essay question

Most essay questions can be answered by framing the specific response around several key words or ideas. Here are a few such key words or ideas:

M's: manpower, materials, methods, money, management
P's: purpose, program, policy, plan, procedure, practice, problems, pitfalls, personnel, public relations

   a. Six basic steps in handling problems:
      1. Preliminary plan and background development
      2. Collect information, data and facts
      3. Analyze and interpret information, data and facts
      4. Analyze and develop solutions as well as make recommendations
      5. Prepare report and sell recommendations
      6. Install recommendations and follow up effectiveness

   b. Pitfalls to avoid
      1. *Taking things for granted* – A statement of the situation does not necessarily imply that each of the elements is necessarily true; for example, a complaint may be invalid and biased so that all that can be taken for granted is that a complaint has been registered

2. *Considering only one side of a situation* – Wherever possible, indicate several alternatives and then point out the reasons you selected the best one
3. *Failing to indicate follow up* – Whenever your answer indicates action on your part, make certain that you will take proper follow-up action to see how successful your recommendations, procedures or actions turn out to be
4. *Taking too long in answering any single question* – Remember to time your answers properly

IX. AFTER THE TEST

Scoring procedures differ in detail among civil service jurisdictions although the general principles are the same. Whether the papers are hand-scored or graded by machine we have described, they are nearly always graded by number. That is, the person who marks the paper knows only the number – never the name – of the applicant. Not until all the papers have been graded will they be matched with names. If other tests, such as training and experience or oral interview ratings have been given, scores will be combined. Different parts of the examination usually have different weights. For example, the written test might count 60 percent of the final grade, and a rating of training and experience 40 percent. In many jurisdictions, veterans will have a certain number of points added to their grades.

After the final grade has been determined, the names are placed in grade order and an eligible list is established. There are various methods for resolving ties between those who get the same final grade – probably the most common is to place first the name of the person whose application was received first. Job offers are made from the eligible list in the order the names appear on it. You will be notified of your grade and your rank as soon as all these computations have been made. This will be done as rapidly as possible.

People who are found to meet the requirements in the announcement are called "eligibles." Their names are put on a list of eligible candidates. An eligible's chances of getting a job depend on how high he stands on this list and how fast agencies are filling jobs from the list.

When a job is to be filled from a list of eligibles, the agency asks for the names of people on the list of eligibles for that job. When the civil service commission receives this request, it sends to the agency the names of the three people highest on this list. Or, if the job to be filled has specialized requirements, the office sends the agency the names of the top three persons who meet these requirements from the general list.

The appointing officer makes a choice from among the three people whose names were sent to him. If the selected person accepts the appointment, the names of the others are put back on the list to be considered for future openings.

That is the rule in hiring from all kinds of eligible lists, whether they are for typist, carpenter, chemist, or something else. For every vacancy, the appointing officer has his choice of any one of the top three eligibles on the list. This explains why the person whose name is on top of the list sometimes does not get an appointment when some of the persons lower on the list do. If the appointing officer chooses the second or third eligible, the No. 1 eligible does not get a job at once, but stays on the list until he is appointed or the list is terminated.

X. HOW TO PASS THE INTERVIEW TEST

The examination for which you applied requires an oral interview test. You have already taken the written test and you are now being called for the interview test – the final part of the formal examination.

You may think that it is not possible to prepare for an interview test and that there are no procedures to follow during an interview. Our purpose is to point out some things you can do in advance that will help you and some good rules to follow and pitfalls to avoid while you are being interviewed.

What is an interview supposed to test?

The written examination is designed to test the technical knowledge and competence of the candidate; the oral is designed to evaluate intangible qualities, not readily measured otherwise, and to establish a list showing the relative fitness of each candidate – as measured against his competitors – for the position sought. Scoring is not on the basis of "right" and "wrong," but on a sliding scale of values ranging from "not passable" to "outstanding." As a matter of fact, it is possible to achieve a relatively low score without a single "incorrect" answer because of evident weakness in the qualities being measured.

Occasionally, an examination may consist entirely of an oral test – either an individual or a group oral. In such cases, information is sought concerning the technical knowledges and abilities of the candidate, since there has been no written examination for this purpose. More commonly, however, an oral test is used to supplement a written examination.

Who conducts interviews?

The composition of oral boards varies among different jurisdictions. In nearly all, a representative of the personnel department serves as chairman. One of the members of the board may be a representative of the department in which the candidate would work. In some cases, "outside experts" are used, and, frequently, a businessman or some other representative of the general public is asked to serve. Labor and management or other special groups may be represented. The aim is to secure the services of experts in the appropriate field.

However the board is composed, it is a good idea (and not at all improper or unethical) to ascertain in advance of the interview who the members are and what groups they represent. When you are introduced to them, you will have some idea of their backgrounds and interests, and at least you will not stutter and stammer over their names.

What should be done before the interview?

While knowledge about the board members is useful and takes some of the surprise element out of the interview, there is other preparation which is more substantive. It *is* possible to prepare for an oral interview – in several ways:

1) Keep a copy of your application and review it carefully before the interview

This may be the only document before the oral board, and the starting point of the interview. Know what education and experience you have listed there, and the sequence and dates of all of it. Sometimes the board will ask you to review the highlights of your experience for them; you should not have to hem and haw doing it.

2) Study the class specification and the examination announcement

Usually, the oral board has one or both of these to guide them. The qualities, characteristics or knowledges required by the position sought are stated in these documents. They offer valuable clues as to the nature of the oral interview. For example, if the job involves supervisory responsibilities, the announcement will usually indicate that knowledge of modern supervisory methods and the qualifications of the candidate as a supervisor will be tested. If so, you can expect such questions, frequently in the form of a hypothetical situation which you are expected to solve. NEVER go into an oral without knowledge of the duties and responsibilities of the job you seek.

3) Think through each qualification required

Try to visualize the kind of questions you would ask if you were a board member. How well could you answer them? Try especially to appraise your own knowledge and background in each area, *measured against the job sought*, and identify any areas in which you are weak. Be critical and realistic – do not flatter yourself.

4) Do some general reading in areas in which you feel you may be weak

For example, if the job involves supervision and your past experience has NOT, some general reading in supervisory methods and practices, particularly in the field of human relations, might be useful. Do NOT study agency procedures or detailed manuals. The oral board will be testing your understanding and capacity, not your memory.

5) Get a good night's sleep and watch your general health and mental attitude

You will want a clear head at the interview. Take care of a cold or any other minor ailment, and of course, no hangovers.

What should be done on the day of the interview?

Now comes the day of the interview itself. Give yourself plenty of time to get there. Plan to arrive somewhat ahead of the scheduled time, particularly if your appointment is in the fore part of the day. If a previous candidate fails to appear, the board might be ready for you a bit early. By early afternoon an oral board is almost invariably behind schedule if there are many candidates, and you may have to wait. Take along a book or magazine to read, or your application to review, but leave any extraneous material in the waiting room when you go in for your interview. In any event, relax and compose yourself.

The matter of dress is important. The board is forming impressions about you – from your experience, your manners, your attitude, and your appearance. Give your personal appearance careful attention. Dress your best, but not your flashiest. Choose conservative, appropriate clothing, and be sure it is immaculate. This is a business interview, and your appearance should indicate that you regard it as such. Besides, being well groomed and properly dressed will help boost your confidence.

Sooner or later, someone will call your name and escort you into the interview room. *This is it.* From here on you are on your own. It is too late for any more preparation. But remember, you asked for this opportunity to prove your fitness, and you are here because your request was granted.

What happens when you go in?

The usual sequence of events will be as follows: The clerk (who is often the board stenographer) will introduce you to the chairman of the oral board, who will introduce you to the other members of the board. Acknowledge the introductions before you sit down. Do not be surprised if you find a microphone facing you or a stenotypist sitting by. Oral interviews are usually recorded in the event of an appeal or other review.

Usually the chairman of the board will open the interview by reviewing the highlights of your education and work experience from your application – primarily for the benefit of the other members of the board, as well as to get the material into the record. Do not interrupt or comment unless there is an error or significant misinterpretation; if that is the case, do not hesitate. But do not quibble about insignificant matters. Also, he will usually ask you some question about your education, experience or your present job – partly to get you to start talking and to establish the interviewing "rapport." He may start the actual questioning, or turn it over to one of the other members. Frequently, each member undertakes the questioning on a particular area, one in which he is perhaps most competent, so you can expect each member to participate in the examination. Because time is limited, you may also expect some rather abrupt switches in the direction the questioning takes, so do not be upset by it. Normally, a board member will not pursue a single line of questioning unless he discovers a particular strength or weakness.

After each member has participated, the chairman will usually ask whether any member has any further questions, then will ask you if you have anything you wish to add. Unless you are expecting this question, it may floor you. Worse, it may start you off on an extended, extemporaneous speech. The board is not usually seeking more information. The question is principally to offer you a last opportunity to present further qualifications or to indicate that you have nothing to add. So, if you feel that a significant qualification or characteristic has been overlooked, it is proper to point it out in a sentence or so. Do not compliment the board on the thoroughness of their examination – they have been sketchy, and you know it. If you wish, merely say, "No thank you, I have nothing further to add." This is a point where you can "talk yourself out" of a good impression or fail to present an important bit of information. Remember, *you close the interview yourself.*

The chairman will then say, "That is all, Mr. _____, thank you." Do not be startled; the interview is over, and quicker than you think. Thank him, gather your belongings and take your leave. Save your sigh of relief for the other side of the door.

How to put your best foot forward
Throughout this entire process, you may feel that the board individually and collectively is trying to pierce your defenses, seek out your hidden weaknesses and embarrass and confuse you. Actually, this is not true. They are obliged to make an appraisal of your qualifications for the job you are seeking, and they want to see you in your best light. Remember, they must interview all candidates and a non-cooperative candidate may become a failure in spite of their best efforts to bring out his qualifications. Here are 15 suggestions that will help you:

1) Be natural – Keep your attitude confident, not cocky
If you are not confident that you can do the job, do not expect the board to be. Do not apologize for your weaknesses, try to bring out your strong points. The board is interested in a positive, not negative, presentation. Cockiness will antagonize any board member and make him wonder if you are covering up a weakness by a false show of strength.

2) Get comfortable, but don't lounge or sprawl
Sit erectly but not stiffly. A careless posture may lead the board to conclude that you are careless in other things, or at least that you are not impressed by the importance of the occasion. Either conclusion is natural, even if incorrect. Do not fuss with your clothing, a pencil or an ashtray. Your hands may occasionally be useful to emphasize a point; do not let them become a point of distraction.

3) Do not wisecrack or make small talk
This is a serious situation, and your attitude should show that you consider it as such. Further, the time of the board is limited – they do not want to waste it, and neither should you.

4) Do not exaggerate your experience or abilities

In the first place, from information in the application or other interviews and sources, the board may know more about you than you think. Secondly, you probably will not get away with it. An experienced board is rather adept at spotting such a situation, so do not take the chance.

5) If you know a board member, do not make a point of it, yet do not hide it

Certainly you are not fooling him, and probably not the other members of the board. Do not try to take advantage of your acquaintanceship – it will probably do you little good.

6) Do not dominate the interview

Let the board do that. They will give you the clues – do not assume that you have to do all the talking. Realize that the board has a number of questions to ask you, and do not try to take up all the interview time by showing off your extensive knowledge of the answer to the first one.

7) Be attentive

You only have 20 minutes or so, and you should keep your attention at its sharpest throughout. When a member is addressing a problem or question to you, give him your undivided attention. Address your reply principally to him, but do not exclude the other board members.

8) Do not interrupt

A board member may be stating a problem for you to analyze. He will ask you a question when the time comes. Let him state the problem, and wait for the question.

9) Make sure you understand the question

Do not try to answer until you are sure what the question is. If it is not clear, restate it in your own words or ask the board member to clarify it for you. However, do not haggle about minor elements.

10) Reply promptly but not hastily

A common entry on oral board rating sheets is "candidate responded readily," or "candidate hesitated in replies." Respond as promptly and quickly as you can, but do not jump to a hasty, ill-considered answer.

11) Do not be peremptory in your answers

A brief answer is proper – but do not fire your answer back. That is a losing game from your point of view. The board member can probably ask questions much faster than you can answer them.

12) Do not try to create the answer you think the board member wants

He is interested in what kind of mind you have and how it works – not in playing games. Furthermore, he can usually spot this practice and will actually grade you down on it.

13) Do not switch sides in your reply merely to agree with a board member

Frequently, a member will take a contrary position merely to draw you out and to see if you are willing and able to defend your point of view. Do not start a debate, yet do not surrender a good position. If a position is worth taking, it is worth defending.

14) Do not be afraid to admit an error in judgment if you are shown to be wrong

The board knows that you are forced to reply without any opportunity for careful consideration. Your answer may be demonstrably wrong. If so, admit it and get on with the interview.

15) Do not dwell at length on your present job

The opening question may relate to your present assignment. Answer the question but do not go into an extended discussion. You are being examined for a *new* job, not your present one. As a matter of fact, try to phrase ALL your answers in terms of the job for which you are being examined.

Basis of Rating

Probably you will forget most of these "do's" and "don'ts" when you walk into the oral interview room. Even remembering them all will not ensure you a passing grade. Perhaps you did not have the qualifications in the first place. But remembering them will help you to put your best foot forward, without treading on the toes of the board members.

Rumor and popular opinion to the contrary notwithstanding, an oral board wants you to make the best appearance possible. They know you are under pressure – but they also want to see how you respond to it as a guide to what your reaction would be under the pressures of the job you seek. They will be influenced by the degree of poise you display, the personal traits you show and the manner in which you respond.

ABOUT THIS BOOK

This book contains tests divided into Examination Sections. Go through each test, answering every question in the margin. We have also attached a sample answer sheet at the back of the book that can be removed and used. At the end of each test look at the answer key and check your answers. On the ones you got wrong, look at the right answer choice and learn. Do not fill in the answers first. Do not memorize the questions and answers, but understand the answer and principles involved. On your test, the questions will likely be different from the samples. Questions are changed and new ones added. If you understand these past questions you should have success with any changes that arise. Tests may consist of several types of questions. We have additional books on each subject should more study be advisable or necessary for you. Finally, the more you study, the better prepared you will be. This book is intended to be the last thing you study before you walk into the examination room. Prior study of relevant texts is also recommended. NLC publishes some of these in our Fundamental Series. Knowledge and good sense are important factors in passing your exam. Good luck also helps. So now study this Passbook, absorb the material contained within and take that knowledge into the examination. Then do your best to pass that exam.

EXAMINATION SECTION

EXAMINATION SECTION
TEST 1

DIRECTIONS: Each question or incomplete statement is followed by several suggested answers or completions. Select the one that BEST answers the question or completes the statement. *PRINT THE LETTER OF THE CORRECT ANSWER IN THE SPACE AT THE RIGHT.*

1. As a clerk in an office in a city agency, you have just been given a new assignment by your supervisor. The assignment was previously done by another clerk.
Before beginning work on this assignment, it is MOST important that you

   A. find out who did the assignment previously
   B. understand your supervisor's instructions for doing the assignment
   C. notify the other clerks in the office that you have just received a new assignment
   D. understand how the assignment is related to the work of other clerks in the office

1.____

2. Assume that you are a clerk in a city department. Your supervisor has given you an important job that he wants completed as quickly as possible. You will be unable to complete the job by the end of the day, and you will be unable to work on the job in the next several days because you will be away from the office.
Of the following, the MOST appropriate action for you to take before leaving the office at the end of the day is to

   A. lock your work in your desk so that the work will not be disturbed
   B. ask another clerk in the office to finish the job while you are away
   C. tell your supervisor how much of the job has been done and how much remains to be done
   D. leave a note on your supervisor's desk, advising him that you will continue to work on the job as soon as you return to the office

2.____

3. Assume that, as a newly appointed clerk in a city department, you are doing an assignment according to a method that your supervisor has told you to use. You believe that you would be less likely to make errors if you were to do the assignment by a different method, although the method your supervisor has told you to use is faster.
For you to discuss your method with your supervisor would be

   A. *desirable* because he may not know the value of your method
   B. *undesirable* because he may know of your method and may prefer the faster one
   C. *desirable* because your method may show your supervisor that you are able to do accurate work
   D. *undesirable* because your method may not be as helpful to you as you believe it to be

3.____

4. Assume that you are responsible for receiving members of the public who visit your department for information. At a time when there are several persons seeking information, a man asks you for information in a rude and arrogant manner. Of the following, the BEST action for you to take in handling this man is to

   A. give him the information in the same manner in which he spoke to you
   B. ignore his request until he asks for the information in a more polite manner

4.____

C. give him the information politely, without commenting to him on his manner
D. ask him to request the information in a polite manner so as not to annoy other people seeking information

5. As a clerk in a city agency, you are assigned to issue publications to members of the public who request the applications in person. Your supervisor has told you that under no circumstances are you to issue more than one application to each person. A person enters the office and asks for two applications, explaining that he wants the second one for use in the event that he makes an error in filling out the application.
Of the following, the MOST appropriate action for you to take in this situation is to

   A. give the person two applications since he may not know how to fill out the application
   B. ask your supervisor for permission to give the person two applications
   C. give one application to the person and advise him to come back later for another one
   D. issue one application to the person and inform him that only one application may be issued to an individual

6. Suppose that as a clerk in an office of a city department, you have been assigned by your supervisor to assist Mr. Jones, another clerk in the office, and to do his work in his absence. Part of Mr. Jones' duties are to give routine information to visitors who request the information. Several months later, shortly after Mr. Jones has begun a three-week vacation, a visitor enters the office and asks for some routine information which is available to the public. He explains that he previously had gotten similar information from Mr. Jones.
Of the following, the MOST advisable action for you to take is to

   A. inform the visitor that Mr. Jones is on vacation but that you will attempt to obtain the information
   B. advise the visitor to return to the office when Mr. Jones will have returned from vacation
   C. tell the visitor that you will have Mr. Jones mail him the information as soon as he returns from vacation
   D. attempt to contact Mr. Jones to ask him whether the information should be given to the visitor

7. Miss Smith is a clerk in the information section of a city department.
Of the following, the MOST desirable way for Miss Smith to answer a telephone call to the section is to say,

   A. "Hello. Miss Smith speaking."
   B. "Miss Smith speaking. May I ask who is calling?"
   C. "Hello. May I be of service to you?"
   D. "Information Section, Miss Smith."

8. When preparing papers for filing, it is NOT desirable to

   A. smooth papers that are wrinkled
   B. use paper clips to keep related papers together in the files
   C. arrange the papers in the order in which they will be filed
   D. mend torn papers with cellophane tape

9. Assume that you are a clerk in the mail room of a city department. One of your duties is to open the letters addressed to the department and to route them to the appropriate offices. One of the letters you open evidently requires the attention of two different offices in the department.
In this situation, the one of the following which is the BEST action for you to take is to

   A. make two duplicate copies of the letter, send one to each office, and keep the original on file in the mail room
   B. send the letter to one of the offices with a request that the letter be forwarded to the second office
   C. return the letter to the writer with a request that he write separate letters to each of the two offices
   D. request the head of each office to send one of his employees to the mail room to decide what should be done with the letter

10. As a mail clerk in a city department, you are responsible for opening incoming mail and routing the letters to the appropriate offices in the department.
The one of the following situations in which it would be MOST appropriate for you to attach a letter to the envelope in which the letter arrives is when the

   A. name and address of the sender, which are on the envelope, are missing from the letter
   B. letter contains important or confidential information
   C. enclosures the envelope is supposed to contain are missing from the envelope
   D. envelope is not addressed to a specific office in the department

11. In writing a letter, it is important that the letter be paragraphed properly.
Of the following, the CHIEF value of proper paragraphing is to

   A. shorten the contents of the letter
   B. assist the writer by shortening the time required to write the letter
   C. aid the reader to understand the contents of the letter more readily
   D. reduce the time required to type the letter

12. A mailing list is a list containing the names and addresses of the individuals and organizations with which a public agency corresponds frequently. Such a list is sometimes kept on 3"x5" cards.
Of the following, the MOST important reason for an agency to keep its mailing list on cards is that

   A. the mailing list changes frequently
   B. more than one office in the agency uses the mailing list
   C. the mailing list is used frequently
   D. only part of the mailing list is used at any one time

13. Under a subject filing system, letters are filed in folders labeled according to subject matter. Assume that you have been asked to file a large number of letters under such a filing system.
Of the following, the FIRST step that you should take in filing these letters is to

   A. arrange the letters alphabetically under each subject
   B. determine under which subject each letter is to be filed

C. arrange the letters by date under each subject
D. prepare cross-references for each letter that should be filed under more than one subject

14. Your supervisor assigns you to file a number of letters in an alphabetical file drawer. In the course of your work, you notice that several letters in the file have been unintentionally misfiled.
Of the following, the MOST appropriate action for you to take in this situation is to

   A. complete your filing assignment and then go through the file again to pick out any misfiled letters for refiling
   B. leave the misfiled letters where they are in order to avoid disturbing the order of the file
   C. put the misfiled letters in their proper places as you discover these letters
   D. insert a note in the misfiled letters' proper places indicating where the misfiled letters may be found

15. Suppose that your supervisor gives you a folder containing a large number of letters arranged in the order of the dates they were received and a list of names of persons in alphabetical order. He asks you to determine, without disturbing the order of the letters, if there is a letter in the folder from each person on the list.
Of the following, the BEST method to use in doing this assignment is to

   A. determine whether the number of letters in the folder is the same as the number of names on the list
   B. look at each letter to see who wrote it, and then place a light check mark on each letter that has been written by a person on the list
   C. prepare a list of the names of the writers of the letters that are in the folder, and then place a light check mark next to each of the names on this list if the name appears on the list of persons your supervisor gave you
   D. look at each letter to see who wrote it, and then place a light check mark next to the name of the person on the list who wrote the letter

16. Whenever material is requested from a file under which the material is filed according to subject, the person requesting the material should be required to make out a requisition slip.
Of the following, the information that ordinarily would be LEAST useful to include on such a requisition slip is the

   A. subject of the material requested
   B. date the material is requested
   C. reason why the material is being requested
   D. name of the person requesting the material

17. A tickler file is GENERALLY used

   A. as a reminder of work to be done
   B. to store inactive records
   C. as an index of the records contained in a filing system
   D. to store miscellaneous important records

18. A listing adding machine prints, on a roll or strip of paper, the numbers added and their sum.
Of the following, the CHIEF advantage of printing the numbers and their sum on the strip of paper is to

     A. provide a check on the accuracy of the machine
     B. show that the addition was done by machine
     C. permit the machine operator to make hand-written corrections in the numbers and their sum
     D. provide a record of the numbers and their sum

18._____

Questions 19-21.

DIRECTIONS: Questions 19 to 21 are to be answered SOLELY on the basis of the information contained in the following paragraph.

In order to organize records properly, it is necessary to start from their very beginning and to trace each copy of the record to find out how it is used, how long it is used, and what may finally be done with it. Although several copies of the record are made, one copy should be marked as the copy of record. This is the formal legal copy, held to meet the requirements of the law. The other copies may be retained for brief periods for reference purposes, but these copies should not be kept after their usefulness as reference ends. There is another reason for tracing records through the office and that is to determine how long it takes the copy of record to reach the central file. The copy of record must not be kept longer than necessary by the section of the office which has prepared it, but should be sent to the central file as soon as possible so that it can be available to the various sections of the office. The central file can make the copy of record available to the various sections of the office at an early date only if it arrives at the central file as quickly as possible. Just as soon as its immediate or active service period is ended, the copy of record should be removed from the central file and put into the inactive file in the office to be stored for whatever length of time may be necessary to meet legal requirements, and then destroyed.

19. According to the above paragraph, a reason for tracing records through an office is to

     A. determine how long the central file must keep the records
     B. organize records properly
     C. find out how many copies of each record are required
     D. identify the copy of record

19._____

20. According to the above paragraph, in order for the central file to have the copy of record available as soon as possible for the various sections of the office, it is MOST important that the

     A. copy of record to be sent to the central file meets the requirements of the law
     B. copy of record is not kept in the inactive file too long
     C. section preparing the copy of record does not unduly delay in sending it to the central file
     D. central file does not keep the copy of record beyond its active service period

20._____

21. According to the above paragraph, the length of time a copy of a record is kept in the inactive file of an office depends CHIEFLY on the   21.____

    A. requirements of the law
    B. length of time that is required to trace the copy of record through the office
    C. use that is made of the copy of record
    D. length of the period that the copy of record is used for reference purposes

22. As a clerk, you may be assigned the duty of opening and sorting the mail coming to your department.   22.____
    The one of the following which is the BEST reason for not discarding the envelopes in which letters come from members of the public until you have glanced at the letters is that

    A. it is rarely necessary to return a letter to the writer in the original envelope
    B. the subject of a letter can, of course, be determined only from the letter itself
    C. the envelopes should usually be filed together with the letters
    D. members of the public frequently neglect to include a return address in their letters

23. Suppose that your supervisor has asked you and another clerk to proofread a letter. The other clerk is reading rapidly to you from the original copy while you are checking the letter.   23.____
    For you to interrupt his reading and make an immediate notation of each error you find is

    A. *wise;* you might otherwise overlook an error
    B. *foolish;* such action slows down the reading
    C. *foolish;* such action demonstrates that the copy is not accurate
    D. *wise;* such action demonstrates that the rate of reading may be increased

24. Suppose that the name files in your office contain filing guides on which appear the letters of the alphabet. The letters X, Y, and Z, unlike the other letters of the alphabet, are grouped together and appear on a single guide.   24.____
    Of the following, the BEST reason for combining these three letters into a single filing unit is probably that

    A. provision must be made for expanding the file if that should become necessary
    B. there is usually insufficient room for filing guides towards the end of a long file
    C. the letters X, Y, and Z are at the end of the alphabet
    D. relatively few names begin with these letters of the alphabet

25. You are requested by your supervisor to replace each card you take out of the files with an *out-of-file* slip. The *out-of-file* slip indicates which card has been removed from the file and where the card may be found. Of the following, the CHIEF value of the *out-of-file* slip is that a clerk looking for a card which happens to have been removed by another clerk   25.____

    A. will know that the card has been returned to the file
    B. can substitute the *out-of-file* slip for the original card
    C. will not waste time searching for the card under the impression that it has been misfiled
    D. is not likely to misfile a card he has been using for some other purpose

26. The sum of 284.5, 3016.24, 8.9736, and 94.15 is MOST NEARLY 26._____

   A. 3402.9   B. 3403.0   C. 3403.9   D. 4036.1

27. If 8394.6 is divided by 29.17, the result is MOST NEARLY 27._____

   A. 288   B. 347   C. 2880   D. 3470

28. If two numbers are multiplied together, the result is 3752. If one of the two numbers is 56, the other number is 28._____

   A. 41   B. 15   C. 109   D. 67

29. The sum of the fractions 1/4, 2/3, 3/8, 5/6, and 3/4 is 29._____

   A. 20/33   B. 1 19/24   C. 2 1/4   D. 2 7/8

30. The fraction 7/16 expressed as a decimal is 30._____

   A. .1120   B. .2286   C. .4375   D. .4850

31. If .10 is divided by 50, the result is 31._____

   A. .002   B. .02   C. .2   D. 2

32. The number 60 is 40% of 32._____

   A. 24   B. 84   C. 96   D. 150

33. If 3/8 of a number is 96, the number is 33._____

   A. 132   B. 36   C. 256   D. 156

34. A city department uses an average of 25 10-cent, 35 15-cent, and 350 20-cent postage stamps each day. The total cost of stamps used by the department in a five-day period is 34._____

   A. $14.75   B. $77.75   C. $145.25   D. $388.75

35. A city department issued 12,000 applications in 2007. The number of applications that the department issued in 2005 was 25% greater than the number it issued in 2007. If the department issued 10% fewer applications in 2003 than it did in 2005, the number it issued in 2003 was 35._____

   A. 16,500   B. 13,500   C. 9,900   D. 8,100

36. A clerk can add 40 columns of figures an hour by using an adding machine and 20 columns of figures an hour without using an adding machine.
The total number of hours it would take him to add 200 columns if he does 3/5 of the work by machine and the rest without the machine is 36._____

   A. 6   B. 7   C. 8   D. 9

37. In 2004, a city department bought 500 dozen pencils at 40 cents per dozen. In 2007, only 75% as many pencils were bought as were bought in 2004, but the price was 20% higher than the 2004 price.
The total cost of the pencils bought in 2007 was 37._____

   A. $180   B. $187.50   C. $240   D. $250

38. A clerk is assigned to check the accuracy of the entries on 490 forms. He checks 40 forms an hour. After working one hour on this task, he is joined by another clerk, who checks these forms at the rate of 35 an hour.
The total number of hours required to do the entire assignment is

   A. 5   B. 6   C. 7   D. 8

39. Assume that there are a total of 420 employees in a city agency. Thirty percent of the employees are clerks, and 1/7 are typists.
The difference between the number of clerks and the number of typists is

   A. 126   B. 66   C. 186   D. 80

40. Assume that a duplicating machine produces copies of a bulletin at a cost of 2 cents per copy. The machine produces 120 copies of the bulletin per minute.
If the cost of producing a certain number of copies was $12, how many minutes of operation did it take the machine to produce this number of copies?

   A. 5   B. 2   C. 10   D. 6

KEY (CORRECT ANSWERS)

1. B	11. C	21. A	31. A
2. C	12. A	22. D	32. D
3. A	13. B	23. A	33. C
4. C	14. C	24. D	34. D
5. D	15. D	25. C	35. B
6. A	16. C	26. C	36. B
7. D	17. A	27. A	37. A
8. B	18. D	28. D	38. C
9. B	19. B	29. D	39. B
10. A	20. C	30. C	40. A

TEST 2

DIRECTIONS: Each question or incomplete statement is followed by several suggested answers or completions. Select the one that BEST answers the question or completes the statement. *PRINT THE LETTER OF THE CORRECT ANSWER IN THE SPACE AT THE RIGHT.*

Questions 1-13.

DIRECTIONS: Each of Questions 1 to 13 consists of a word in capitals followed by four suggested meanings of the word. For each question, indicate in the correspondingly numbered space at the right the letter preceding the word which means MOST NEARLY the same as the word in capitals.

1. AUTHORIZE
    A. write B. permit C. request D. recommend

2. ASSESS
    A. set a value on B. belong
    C. think highly of D. increase

3. CONVENTIONAL
    A. democratic B. convenient C. modern D. customary

4. DEPLETE
    A. replace B. exhaust C. review D. withhold

5. INTERVENE
    A. sympathize with B. differ
    C. ask for an opinion D. interfere

6. HAZARDOUS
    A. dangerous B. unusual C. slow D. difficult

7. SUBSTANTIATE
    A. replace B. suggest C. verify D. suffer

8. DISCORD
    A. remainder B. disagreement C. pressure D. dishonest

9. TENACIOUS
    A. vicious B. irritable C. truthful D. unyielding

10. ALLEVIATE
    A. relieve B. appreciate C. succeed D. admit

11. FALLACY
    A. basis B. false idea
    C. guilt D. lack of respect

12. SCRUTINIZE 12.___
     A. reject   B. bring about   C. examine   D. insist upon

13. IMMINENT 13.___
     A. anxious   B. well-known   C. important   D. about to happen

Questions 14-25.

DIRECTIONS: Each of Questions 14 to 25 consists of a sentence which may be classified appropriately under one of the following four categories:
A. incorrect because of faulty grammar or sentence structure
B. incorrect because of faulty punctuation
C. incorrect because of faulty capitalization
D. correct

Examine each sentence carefully. Then, in the correspondingly numbered space at the right, indicate the letter preceding the category which is the BEST of the four suggested above. Each incorrect sentence contains only one type of error. Consider a sentence correct if it contains no errors, although there may be other correct ways of expressing the same thought.

14. All the clerks, including those who have been appointed recently are required to work on the new assignment. 14.___

15. The office manager asked each employee to work one Saturday a month. 15.___

16. Neither Mr. Smith nor Mr. Jones was able to finish his assignment on time. 16.___

17. The task of filing these cards is to be divided equally between you and he. 17.___

18. He is an employee whom we consider to be efficient. 18.___

19. I believe that the new employees are not as punctual as us. 19.___

20. The employees, working in this office, are to be congratulated for their work. 20.___

21. The supervisor entered the room and said, "The work must be completed today." 21.___

22. The employees were given their assignments and, they were asked to begin work immediately. 22.___

23. The letter will be sent to the United States senate this week. 23.___

24. When the supervisor entered the room, he noticed that the book was laying on the desk. 24.___

25. The price of the pens were higher than the price of the pencils. 25.___

Questions 26-35.

DIRECTIONS: Each of Questions 26 to 35 consists of a group of four words. One word in each group is INCORRECTLY spelled. For each question, indicate in the correspondingly numbered space at the right, the letter preceding the word which is INCORRECTLY spelled.

26.	A. grateful	B. fundimental	C. census	D. analysis	26.____
27.	A. installment	B. retrieve	C. concede	D. dissapear	27.____
28.	A. accidentaly	B. dismissal	C. conscientious	D. indelible	28.____
29.	A. perceive	B. carreer	C. anticipate	D. acquire	29.____
30.	A. facillity	B. reimburse	C. assortment	D. guidance	30.____
31.	A. plentiful	B. across	C. advantagous	D. similar	31.____
32.	A. omission	B. pamphlet	C. guarrantee	D. repel	32.____
33.	A. maintenance	B. always	C. liable	D. anouncement	33.____
34.	A. exaggerate	B. sieze	C. condemn	D. commit	34.____
35.	A. pospone	B. altogether	C. grievance	D. excessive	35.____

Questions 36-41.

DIRECTIONS: Questions 36 to 41 are to be answered SOLELY on the basis of the information and directions given below.

Assume that you are a clerk assigned to the personnel bureau of a department. Your supervisor has asked you to classify the employees in your agency into the following four groups:

    A. Female employees who are college graduates, who are less than 35 years of age, and who earn at least $36,000 a year;
    B. Male employees who are not college graduates, who are less than 35 years of age, and who earn at least $38,000 a year but not more than $44,000 a year;
    C. Female employees who are 35 years of age or older, who are not college graduates, and who earn at least $30,000 a year but less than $36,000 a year;
    D. Male employees who are college graduates, who are 35 years of age or older, and who earn more than $44,000 a year.

NOTE: In each question, consider only the information which will assist you in classifying each employee. Any information which is of no assistance in classifying an employee should not be considered.

SAMPLE: Mr. Smith, a city resident, is 60 years of age, and is a college graduate. His salary is $45,600 a year.

The correct answer to this sample is D, since the employee is a male college graduate, is more than 35 years of age, and earns more than $44,000 a year.

Questions 36 to 41 contain information from the personnel records in the department. For each question, indicate in the correspondingly numbered space at the right the letter preceding the appropriate group into which you would place each employee.

36. Mrs. Brown is a 33-year-old accountant who was graduated from college with honors. Her present annual salary is $43,480.   36.____

37. Mr. Queen has had two promotions since beginning work for the department eight years ago at the age of 29. A college graduate, he receives $50,800 a year as supervisor in charge of a bureau.

37.____

38. Miss Arthur earns $35,400 a year and has worked in the department for five years. Now 36 years of age, she attends high school in the evenings and hopes to obtain a high school diploma.

38.____

39. At 34 years of age, Mr. Smith earns $43,960 per annum. After he was graduated from high school, he attended college for two years, but he did not complete his college course.

39.____

40. Mr. Rose is a 28-year-old high school graduate earning $38,200 a year. He intends to attend college in the evenings to study public administration.

40.____

41. Mr. Johnson, a veteran, attended college in the evenings for six years before he obtained a degree in engineering. At 37 years of age, he earns an annual salary of $53,200.

41.____

Questions 42-50.

DIRECTIONS: Each of Questions 42 to 50 consists of four names. For each question, select the one of the four names that should be THIRD if the four names were arranged in alphabetical order in accordance with the Rules of Alphabetical Filing given below. Read these rules carefully. Then, for each question indicate in the correspondingly numbered space at the right the letter preceding the name that should be THIRD in alphabetical order.

RULES FOR ALPHABETICAL FILING

NAMES OF INDIVIDUALS

(1) The names of individuals are filed in strict alphabetical order: first according to the last name, then according to first name or initial, and finally according to middle name or initial. For example: William Jones precedes George Kirk, and Arthur S. Blake precedes Charles M. Blake.

(2) When the last names are identical, the one with an initial instead of a first name precedes the one with a first name beginning with the same initial. For example: J. Green precedes Joseph Green.

(3) When identical last names also have identical first names, the one without a middle name or initial precedes the one with a middle name or initial. For example: Robert Jackson precedes both Robert C. Jackson and Robert Chester Jackson.

(4) When last names are identical and the first names are also identical, the one with a middle initial precedes the one with a middle name beginning with the same initial. For example: Peter A. Brown precedes Peter Alvin Brown.

(5) Prefixes such as De, El, La, and Van are considered parts of the names they precede. For example: Wilfred De Wald precedes Alexander Duval.

(6) Last names beginning with "Mac" or "Mc" are filed as spelled.

(7)   Abbreviated names are treated as if they were spelled out. For example: Jos. is filed as Joseph, and Robt. is filed as Robert.

(8)   Titles and designations such as Dr., Mrs., Prof. are disregarded in filing.

NAMES OF BUSINESS ORGANIZATIONS

(1)   The names of business organisations are filed exactly as written, except that an organization bearing the name of an individual is filed alphabetically according to the name of the individual in accordance with the rules for filing names of individuals given above. For example: Thomas Allison Machine Company precedes Northern Baking Company.

(2)   When numerals occur in a name, they are treated as if they were spelled out. For example: 6 stands for six, and 4th stands for fourth.

(3)   When the following words occur in names, they are disregarded: the, of, and.

SAMPLE:
- A.   Fred Town   (2)
- B.   Jack Towne   (3)
- C.   D. Town   (1)
- D.   Jack S. Towne   (4)

The numbers in parentheses indicate the proper alphabetical order in which these names should be filed. Since the name that should be filed THIRD is Jack Towne, the answer is B.

42.
- A. Herbert Restman
- B. H. Restman
- C. Harry Restmore
- D. H. Restmore

43.
- A. Martha Eastwood
- B. Martha E. Eastwood
- C. Martha Edna Eastwood
- D. M. Eastwood

44.
- A. Timothy Macalan
- B. Fred McAlden
- C. Thomas MacAllister
- D. Mrs. Frank McAllen

45.
- A. Elm Trading Co.
- B. El Dorado Trucking Corp.
- C. James Eldred Jewelry Store
- D. Eldridge Printing, Inc.

46.
- A. Edward La Gabriel
- B. Marie Doris Gabriel
- C. Marjorie N. Gabriel
- D. Marjorie N. Gabriel

47. A. Peter La Vance
     B. George Van Meer
     C. Wallace De Vance
     D. Leonard Vance

48. A. Fifth Avenue Book Shop
     B. Mr. Wm. A. Fifner
     C. 52nd Street Association
     D. Robert B. Fiffner

49. A. Dr. Chas. D. Peterson
     B. Miss Irene F. Petersen
     C. Lawrence E. Peterson
     D. Prof. N.A. Petersen

50. A. 71st Street Theater
     B. The Seven Seas Corp.
     C. 7th Ave. Service Co.
     D. Walter R. Sevan and Co.

47. ___
48. ___
49. ___
50. ___

KEY (CORRECT ANSWERS)

1. B	11. B	21. D	31. C	41. D
2. A	12. C	22. B	32. C	42. D
3. D	13. D	23. C	33. D	43. B
4. B	14. B	24. A	34. B	44. B
5. D	15. C	25. A	35. A	45. D
6. A	16. D	26. B	36. A	46. C
7. C	17. A	27. D	37. D	47. D
8. B	18. D	28. A	38. C	48. A
9. D	19. A	29. B	39. B	49. A
10. A	20. B	30. A	40. B	50. C

EXAMINATION SECTION
TEST 1

DIRECTIONS: Each question or incomplete statement is followed by several suggested answers or completions. Select the one that BEST answers the question or completes the statement. *PRINT THE LETTER OF THE CORRECT ANSWER IN THE SPACE AT THE RIGHT.*

1. Assume that you are appointed as a clerk in a city department. As a new employee, you are PRIMARILY expected to

    A. inform your supervisor of the amount of training you will need to handle your new job
    B. perform your work in accordance with the instructions given you by your supervisor
    C. show your supervisor that you like the work you are assigned to do
    D. prove to your supervisor that you are able to handle your new job with very little instruction

    1.____

2. Assume that you are a clerk in a city agency. One day, your supervisor tells you that he will be too busy to speak to visitors coming to the office that day. He instructs you to refer all visitors, including those with urgent business, to Mr. Brown, one of his assistants. During the day, a visitor enters the office and tells you that he wishes to speak to your supervisor on an important matter. Of the following, the MOST appropriate course of action for you to take in this situation is to

    A. advise the visitor that Mr. Brown may be better informed than your supervisor on the matter
    B. notify your supervisor that a visitor wishes to speak to him on an important matter
    C. ask the visitor to return at another time when your supervisor will be able to speak to him
    D. inform the visitor that your supervisor is not available but that Mr. Brown will attempt to help him

    2.____

3. As a clerk in the mail room of a large city department, you are responsible for opening incoming letters and for routing them to the appropriate offices in the department. The MOST important reason why you should know thoroughly the functions of the various offices in the department is that

    A. letters are sometimes addressed only to the department rather than to a specific office in the department
    B. each office may have its own method of answering letters
    C. a letter addressed only to the department would not have to be opened before forwarding it to the proper office
    D. an accurate listing of the locations of offices and employees in the department is essential to a mail room clerk

    3.____

4. Suppose that one of your duties as a clerk in a city department is to answer letters requesting information. One such letter requests some information that you can supply immediately and other information which you know will not be available for several weeks. It is evident that the writer of the letter is not aware that some of the information is not available immediately.
Of the following, the MOST appropriate action for you to take in this matter is to

    4.____

A. supply the writer with the information that is available immediately and ask him to write for the rest of the information at a later date
B. supply the writer with the information that is available immediately and inform him that the rest of the information will be sent in several weeks
C. write to the person requesting the information, asking him to make his request again in several weeks when all the information will be available
D. wait until the rest of the information becomes available in several weeks and then send all the information at once

5. Assume that you have been given an unalphabetized list of 1,000 employees in your agency and a set of unalphabetized payroll cards. You have been asked to determine if, for each name on the list, there is a corresponding payroll card.
Of the following, the BEST reason for first alphabetizing the payroll cards is that

A. each name on the list could then be more easily checked against the payroll cards
B. it then becomes easier to alphabetize the names on the list
C. introducing an additional step in the checking process produces a more complicated procedure
D. you may obtain additional information from the payroll cards to help you check the names

6. Suppose that you have just been appointed as a clerk in a city department. Although your supervisor has given you instructions for filing personnel cards, you still do not fully understand how to file them.
For you to ask your supervisor to explain more fully how you are to file the cards would be desirable CHIEFLY because

A. you will prove to your supervisor that you intend to do a good job
B. your supervisor will be willing to explain the instructions more fully
C. you will be better prepared to do the assignment if you fully understand what you are to do
D. new employees cannot be expected to do their work properly without having instructions repeated

7. In many cases, it becomes evident that a filing problem exists only after a paper has been filed and cannot be found.
On the basis of the above statement, it is MOST accurate to state that

A. filing problems become evident before errors in filing have been discovered
B. a filing problem is solved when a misfiled paper is found
C. even a careful file clerk may create a filing problem
D. a filing problem may not become apparent until a filed paper cannot be located

8. Assume that you are a newly appointed clerk in a large office of a city department. You believe that the method used for doing a certain type of work in the office should be changed.
Of the following, the MOST important reason why you should suggest the change to your supervisor is that

A. supervisors are usually reluctant to make changes unless they are necessary
B. you are expected, as a new employee, to suggest important improvements in office work

C. your suggestion may improve the method used for this type of work
D. it is more important to make changes in large offices than in small ones

9. The average citizen is not interested in the amount of work assigned to public employees or the pressure under which they sometimes work. If a public employee fails to give prompt and courteous service, the average citizen estimates the efficiency of all public employees accordingly.
On the basis of the above passage, the MOST accurate of the following statements is that

   A. the average citizen usually realizes that the efficiency of public employees depends upon the amount of work assigned to them
   B. the average citizen's attitude toward all public employees may be influenced by the service rendered by an individual public employee
   C. the pressure of work duties often causes public employees to render unsatisfactory service to the public
   D. the average citizen may help to improve the efficiency of public employees by taking an interest in their work

10. Suppose that you have been asked to proofread a copy of a report with another clerk. The other clerk is to read to you from the original report while you check the copy for errors.
For you to make a notation of each error as you detect it rather than wait until the end of the proofreading to note all the errors at once would be

   A. *desirable;* you would be less likely to overlook noting an error
   B. *undesirable;* the original report may not be correct
   C. *desirable;* the more clearly the other clerk reads, the more accurately you will be able to detect and note errors
   D. *undesirable;* the notations made during the proofreading may not be legible later

11. If the methods used in an office seem to be faulty, an employee should offer constructive suggestions instead of mere criticisms of the methods.
On the basis of this statement, it is MOST accurate to state that

   A. the methods used in an office should be criticized only if they cannot be improved
   B. most of the problems arising in an office can be overcome satisfactorily by employee suggestions
   C. an employee should suggest improvements for existing poor methods rather than only find fault with them
   D. the quality of suggestions submitted by employees depends upon the methods used in an office

12. The abbreviation *e.g.* ORDINARILY means

   A. instead of   B. express charges guaranteed
   C. for example   D. excellent grade

13. As a clerk assigned to keeping payroll records in your department, you are instructed by your supervisor to use a new method for keeping the records. You think that the new method will be less effective than the one you are now using.
In this situation, it would be MOST advisable for you to

A. use the new method to keep the records even if you think it may be less effective
B. continue to use the method you consider to be more effective without saying anything to your supervisor
C. use the method you consider to be more effective and then tell your supervisor your reasons for doing so
D. use the new method only if you can improve its effectiveness

14. The term that describes the programs installed on an office computer is

    A. interface   B. hardware
    C. network   D. software

15. An examination of the financial records of a business firm or public agency in order to determine its true financial condition is called a(n)

    A. budget   B. voucher
    C. audit   D. appropriation

Questions 16-17.

DIRECTIONS: Questions 16 and 17 are to be answered SOLELY on the basis of the information contained in the following statement.

A duplex envelope is an envelope composed of two sections securely fastened together so that they become one mailing piece. This type of envelope makes it possible for a first class letter to be delivered simultaneously with third or fourth class matter and yet not require payment of the much higher first class postage rate on the entire mailing. First class postage is paid only on the letter which goes in the small compartment, third or fourth class postage being paid on the contents of the larger compartment. The larger compartment generally has an ungummed flap or clasp for sealing. The first class or smaller compartment has a gummed flap for sealing. Postal regulations require that the exact amount of postage applicable to each compartment be separately attached to it.

16. On the basis of this paragraph, it is MOST accurate to state that

    A. the smaller compartment is placed inside the larger compartment before mailing
    B. the two compartments may be detached and mailed separately
    C. two classes of mailing matter may be mailed as a unit at two different postage rates
    D. the more expensive postage rate is paid on the matter in the larger compartment

17. When a duplex envelope is used, the

    A. first class compartment may be sealed with a clasp
    B. correct amount of postage must be placed on each compartment
    C. compartment containing third or fourth class mail requires a gummed flap for sealing
    D. full amount of postage for both compartments may be placed on the larger compartment

18. The MOST accurate of the following statements is that a City Charter

    A. lists the names, titles, and salaries of the heads of the various city agencies
    B. shows the funds allocated to each city agency

C. contains all the local laws passed by the City Council
D. describes the functions of city agencies

19. A period of inflation may generally BEST be described as a period in which the

    A. hourly and weekly wages paid to employees decline rapidly
    B. purchasing power of pensions and other fixed incomes increases
    C. purchasing power of money declines
    D. number of unemployed persons increases sharply

20. You have been asked by your supervisor to code about 500 cards on each of six different classification bases according to a previously prepared key. Halfway through the task, you realize suddenly that on the last few cards, you have begun to use incorrect code numbers in coding one particular classification. You know that your work will be checked by another clerk.
    For you to go back to the beginning of the cards immediately and to check the coding of only the particular classification in the coding of which you have erred would be commendable CHIEFLY because

    A. all the cards will be checked carefully by another clerk
    B. you have probably misinterpreted the entire coding key
    C. there is an especially strong likelihood of error in the coding of the particular classification
    D. you have almost completed the task and no time will be wasted

21. Suppose that it is the practice in your department to file all the correspondence with one individual in a single folder and to file the most recent letters first in the folder.
    Of the following, the BEST justification for placing the most recent letter first rather than last in the folder is that, in general,

    A. letters placed in front of a folder are usually less accessible
    B. requests for previous correspondence from the files usually concern letters filed relatively recently
    C. letters in a folder can usually be located most quickly when they are filed in a definite order
    D. filing can usually be accomplished very quickly when letters are placed in a folder without reference to date

22. While filing cards in an alphabetical file, you notice a card which is not in its correct alphabetical order.
    Of the following, the BEST action for you to take is to

    A. show the card to your supervisor and ask him whether that card has been reported lost
    B. leave the card where it is, but inform the other clerks who use the file exactly where they may find the card if they need it
    C. file a cross-reference card in the place where the card should have been filed
    D. make a written notation of where you can find the card in the event that your supervisor asks you for it

23. The sum of 637.894, 8352.16, 4.8673, and 301.5 is MOST NEARLY

    A. 8989.5   B. 9021.35   C. 9294.9   D. 9296.4

24. If 30 is divided by .06, the result is

    A. 5 B. 5 C. 500 D. 5000

25. The sum of the fractions 1/3, 4/6, 1/2, 3/4 and 1/12 is

    A. 3 1/4 B. 2 1/3 C. 2 1/6 D. 1 11/12

26. If 96934.42 is divided by 53.496, the result is MOST NEARLY

    A. 181 B. 552 C. 1810 D. 5520

27. If 25% of a number is 48, the number is

    A. 12 B. 60 C. 144 D. 192

28. The average number of reports filed per day by a clerk during a five-day week was 720. He filed 610 reports the first day, 720 reports the second day, 740 reports the third day, and 755 reports the fourth day.
    The number of reports he filed the fifth day was

    A. 748 B. 165 C. 775 D. 565

29. The number 88 is 2/5 of

    A. 123 B. 141 C. 220 D. 440

30. If the product of 8.3 multiplied by .42 is subtracted from the product of 156 multiplied by .09, the result is MOST NEARLY

    A. 10.6 B. 13.7 C. 17.5 D. 20.8

31. A city department employs 1400 people, of whom 35% are clerks and 1/8 are stenographers.
    The number of employees in the department who are neither clerks nor stenographers is

    A. 640 B. 665 C. 735 D. 760

32. Assume that there are 190 papers to be filed and that Clerk A and Clerk B are assigned to file these papers. If Clerk A files 40 papers more than Clerk B, then the number of papers that Clerk A files is

    A. 75 B. 110 C. 115 D. 150

33. A stock clerk had on hand the following items:
    500 pads, each worth four cents
    130 pencils, each worth three cents
    50 dozen rubber bands, worth two cents a dozen
    If, from this stock, he issued 125 pads, 45 pencils, and 48 rubber bands, the value of the remaining stock would be

    A. $6.43 B. $8.95 C. $17.63 D. $18.47

34. An assignment is completed by 32 clerks in 22 days. Assuming that all the clerks work at the same rate of speed, the number of clerks that would be needed to complete this assignment in 16 days is

A. 27   B. 38   C. 44   D. 52

35. A department head hired a total of 60 temporary employees to handle a seasonal increase in the department's workload. The following lists the number of temporary employees hired, their rates of pay, and the duration of their employment:
One-third of the total were hired as clerks, each at the rate of $13,750 a year, for two months
30 percent of the total were hired as office machine operators, each at the rate of $15,750 a year, for four months
22 stenographers were hired, each at the rate of $15,000 a year, for three months
The total amount paid to these temporary employees was MOST NEARLY

   A. $890,000   B. $225,000   C. $325,000   D. $196,000

36. Assume that there are 2300 employees in a city agency. Also assume that five percent of these employees are accountants, that 80 percent of the accountants have college degrees, and that one-half of the accountants who have college degrees have five years of experience.
Then the number of employees in the agency who are accountants with college degrees and five years of experience is

   A. 46   B. 51   C. 460   D. 920

Questions 37-50.

DIRECTIONS: Each of Questions 37 to 50 consists of a word in capitals followed by four suggested meanings of the word. For each question, indicate in the correspondingly numbered space at the right the letter preceding the word which means MOST NEARLY the same as the word in capitals.

37. AUXILIARY
    A. unofficial   B. available   C. temporary   D. aiding

38. DELETE
    A. explain   B. delay   C. erase   D. conceal

39. REFUTE
    A. receive   B. endorse   C. disprove   D. decline

40. CANDID
    A. correct   B. hasty   C. careful   D. frank

41. INFRACTION
    A. violation   B. investigation   C. punishment   D. part

42. OBJECTIVE
    A. method   B. goal   C. importance   D. fault

43. CONCUR
    A. agree   B. demand   C. control   D. create

44. JUSTIFY
    A. defend   B. understand   C. complete   D. request

45. INFER
    A. impress   B. conclude   C. intrude   D. decrease

46. CONSTRUE
    A. suggest   B. predict   C. interpret   D. urge

47. TRIVIAL
    A. unexpected   B. exact   C. unnecessary   D. petty

48. OPTIONAL
    A. useful   B. voluntary   C. valuable   D. obvious

49. SUBSEQUENT
    A. following   B. successful   C. permanent   D. simple

50. REVISE
    A. introduce   B. explain   C. begin   D. change

KEY (CORRECT ANSWERS)

1. B	11. C	21. B	31. C	41. A
2. D	12. C	22. A	32. C	42. B
3. A	13. A	23. D	33. D	43. A
4. B	14. D	24. C	34. C	44. A
5. A	15. C	25. B	35. B	45. B
6. C	16. C	26. C	36. A	46. C
7. D	17. B	27. D	37. D	47. D
8. C	18. D	28. C	38. C	48. B
9. B	19. C	29. C	39. C	49. A
10. A	20. C	30. A	40. D	50. D

TEST 2

DIRECTIONS: Each of Questions 1 to 9 consists of a word in capitals followed by four suggested meanings of the word. For each question, indicate in the correspondingly numbered space at the right the letter preceding the word which means MOST NEARLY the same as the word in capitals.

1. CONCISE
   A. hidden B. complicated C. compact D. recent

2. PROSPECTIVE
   A. anticipated B. patient C. influential D. shrewd

3. STIMULATE
   A. regulate B. arouse C. imitate D. strengthen

4. EXPEDITE
   A. exceed B. expand C. solve D. hasten

5. RENOUNCE
   A. remind B. raise C. reject D. restore

6. SURMISE
   A. inform B. suppose C. convince D. pretend

7. FLUCTUATE
   A. vary B. divide C. improve D. irritate

8. PERTINENT
   A. attractive B. related C. practical D. lasting

9. CENSURE
   A. confess B. count C. confirm D. criticize

Questions 10-14.

DIRECTIONS: Each of Questions 10 to 14 consists of a sentence which may be classified appropriately under one of the following four categories:
    A. incorrect because of faulty grammar or sentence structure
    B. incorrect because of faulty punctuation
    C. incorrect because of faulty capitalization
    D. correct

Examine each sentence carefully. Then, in the correspondingly numbered space at the right, indicate the letter preceding the category which is the BEST of the four suggested above. Each incorrect sentence contains only one type of error. Consider a sentence correct if it contains none of the types of errors mentioned, although there may be other correct ways of expressing the same thought.

10. We have learned that there was more than twelve people present at the meeting. 10.___
11. Every one of the employees is able to do this kind of work. 11.___
12. Neither the supervisor nor his assistant are in the office today. 12.___
13. The office manager announced that any clerk, who volunteered for the assignment, would be rewarded. 13.___
14. After looking carefully in all the files, the letter was finally found on a desk. 14.___
15. In answer to the clerk's question, the supervisor said, "this assignment must be completed today." 15.___
16. The office manager says that he can permit only you and me to go to the meeting. 16.___
17. The supervisor refused to state who he would assign to the reception unit. 17.___
18. At the last meeting, he said that he would interview us in September. 18.___
19. Mr. Jones, who is one of our most experienced employees has been placed in charge of the main office. 19.___
20. I think that this adding machine is the most useful of the two we have in our office. 20.___
21. Between you and I, our new stenographer is not as competent as our former stenographer. 21.___
22. The new assignment should be given to whoever can do the work rapidly. 22.___
23. Mrs. Smith, as well as three other typists, was assigned to the new office. 23.___
24. The staff assembled for the conference on time but, the main speaker arrived late. 24.___

Questions 25-34.

DIRECTIONS: Each of Questions 25 to 34 consists of a group of four words. One word in each group is INCORRECTLY spelled. For each question, indicate in the correspondingly numbered space at the right the letter preceding the word which is INCORRECTLY spelled.

25. A. arguing   B. correspon-dance   C. forfeit   D. dissension   25.___
26. A. occasion   B. description   C. prejudice   D. elegible   26.___
27. A. accomodate   B. initiative   C. changeable   D. enroll   27.___
28. A. temporary   B. insistent   C. benificial   D. separate   28.___
29. A. achieve   B. dissappoint   C. unanimous   D. judgment   29.___

3 (#2)

30.	A.	procede	B.	publicly	C.	sincerity	D.	successful	30.____
31.	A.	deceive	B.	goverment	C.	preferable	D.	repetitive	31.____
32.	A.	emphasis	B.	skillful	C.	advisible	D.	optimistic	32.____
33.	A.	tendency	B.	rescind	C.	crucial	D.	noticable	33.____
34.	A.	privelege	B.	abbreviate	C.	simplify	D.	divisible	34.____

Questions 35-43.

DIRECTIONS: Each of Questions 35 to 43 consists of four names. For each question, select the one of the four names that should be FOURTH if the four names were arranged in alphabetical order in accordance with the Rules for Alphabetical Filing given below. Read these rules carefully. Then, for each question, indicate in the correspondingly numbered space at the right the letter preceding the name that should be FOURTH in alphabetical order.

RULES FOR ALPHABETICAL FILING

NAMES OF INDIVIDUALS

(1) File all names of individuals in strict alphabetical order, first according to the last name, then according to first name or initial, and finally according to middle name or initial. For example: George Brown precedes Edward Hunt, and Charles N. Smith precedes David A. Smith.

(2) Where the last names are identical, the one with an initial instead of a first name precedes the one with a first name beginning with the same initial. For example: G. Brown and G.B. Brown precede George A. Brown.

(3) Where two identical last names also have identical first names or initials, the one without a middle name or initial precedes the one with a middle name or initial. For example: William Jones precedes both William B. Jones and William Bruce Jones.

(4) When two last names are identical and the two first names or initials are also identical, the one with a middle initial precedes the one with a middle name beginning with the same initial. For example: William B. Jones precedes William Bruce Jones.

(5) Prefixes such as D', De, La, and Le are considered parts of the names they precede. For example: George De Gregory precedes Arthur Dempsey.

(6) Last names beginning with "Mac" or "Mc" are to be filed as spelled.

(7) Abbreviated names are to be treated as if they were spelled out. For example: Chas. is filed as Charles, and Wm. is filed as William.

(8) Titles and designations such as Dr., Mr., and Prof, are to be disregarded in filing.

NAMES OF BUSINESS ORGANIZATIONS

(1) File names of business organizations exactly as written, except that an organization bearing the name of an individual is filed alphabetically according to the name of the individual in accordance with the rules for filing names of individuals given above. For example: Samuel Eartnett Lumber Company precedes Mutual Grocery Company.

(2) Where numerals occur in a name, they are to be treated as if they were spelled out. For example: 5 stands for five and 9th stands for ninth.

(3) Where the following words occur in names, they are to be disregarded: the, of, and.

SAMPLE:
    A. William Brown   (2)
    B. Arthur F. Browne   (4)
    C. Arthur Browne   (3)
    D. F. Brown   (1)

The numbers in parentheses indicate the proper alphabetical order in which these names should be filed. Since the name that should be filed FOURTH is Arthur F. Browne, the answer is B.

35.   A. Francis Lattimore   B. H. Latham
     C. G. Lattimore   D. Hugh Latham

36.   A. Thomas B. Morgan   B. Thomas Morgan
     C. T. Morgan   D. Thomas Bertram Morgan

37.   A. Lawrence A. Villon   B. Chas. Valente
     C. Charles M. Valent   D. Lawrence De Villon

38.   A. Alfred Devance   B. A.R. D'Amico
     C. Arnold De Vincent   D. A. De Pino

39.   A. Dr. Milton A. Bergmann   B. Miss Evelyn M. Bergmenn
     C. Prof. E.N. Bergmenn   D. Mrs. L.B. Bergmann

40.   A. George MacDougald   B. Thomas McHern
     C. William Macholt   D. Frank McHenry

41.   A. Third National Bank   B. Robt. Tempkin Corp.
     C. 32nd Street Carpet Co.   D. Wm. Templeton, Inc.

42.   A. Mary Lobell Art Shop   B. John La Marca, Inc.
     C. Lawyers' Guild   D. Frank Le Goff Studios

43.   A. 9th Avenue Garage   B. Jos. Nuren Food Co.
     C. The New Book Store   D. Novelty Card Corp.

Questions 44-50.

DIRECTIONS: Questions 44 to 50 are to be answered on the basis of the following Code Table. In this table, for each number a corresponding code letter is given. Each of the questions contains three pairs of numbers and code letters. In each pair, the code letters should correspond with the numbers in accordance with the Code Table.

CODE TABLE

Number	1	2	3	4	5	6	7	8	9	0
Corresponding Code Letter	Y	N	Z	X	W	T	U	P	S	R

In some of the pairs below, an error exists in the coding. Examine the pairs in each question carefully.
If an error exists in:
  only one of the pairs in the question, mark your answer A
  any two pairs in the question, mark your answer B
  all three pairs in the question, mark your answer C
  none of the pairs in the question, mark your answer D

SAMPLE:
  37258 - ZUNWP
  948764 - SXPTTX
  73196 - UZYSP

In the above sample, the first pair is correct since each number, as listed, has the correct corresponding code letter. In the second pair, an error exists because the number 7 should have the code letter U instead of the letter T. In the third pair, an error exists because the number 6 should have the code letter T instead of the letter P. Since there are errors in two of the three pairs, the correct answer is B.

44. 493785 - XSZUPW
    86398207 - PTUSPNRU
    5943162 - WSXZYTN   44._____

45. 5413968412 - WXYZSTPXYR
    8763451297 - PUTZXWYZSU
    4781965302 - XUPYSUWZRN   45._____

46. 79137584 - USYRUWPX
    638247 - TZPNXS
    49679312 - XSTUSZYN   46._____

47. 37854296 - ZUPWXNST
    09183298 - RSYXZNSP
    91762358 - SYUTNXWP   47._____

48. 3918762485 - ZSYPUTNXPW
    1578291436 - YWUPNSYXZT
    2791385674 - NUSYZPWTUX   48._____

6 (#2)

49. 197546821 - YSUWSTPNY
    873024867 - PUZRNWPTU
    583179246 - WPZYURNXT

50. 510782463 - WYRUSNXTZ
    478192356 - XUPYSNZWT
    961728532 - STYUNPWXN

49. ___

50. ___

KEY (CORRECT ANSWERS)

1. C	11. D	21. A	31. B	41. C
2. A	12. A	22. D	32. C	42. A
3. B	13. B	23. D	33. D	43. B
4. D	14. A	24. B	34. A	44. A
5. C	15. C	25. B	35. C	45. C
6. B	16. D	26. D	36. D	46. B
7. A	17. A	27. A	37. A	47. B
8. B	18. C	28. C	38. C	48. D
9. D	19. B	29. B	39. B	49. C
10. A	20. A	30. A	40. B	50. B

EXAMINATION SECTION
TEST 1

DIRECTIONS: Each question or incomplete statement is followed by several suggested answers or completions. Select the one that BEST answers the question or completes the statement. *PRINT THE LETTER OF THE CORRECT ANSWER IN THE SPACE AT THE RIGHT.*

1. A city employee should realize that in his contacts with the public,

    A. he should always agree with what a visitor says because *the customer is always right*
    B. he should not give any information over the telephone unless the caller identifies himself
    C. the manner in which he treats a visitor may determine the visitor's opinion of government employees generally
    D. visitors should at all times be furnished with all the information they request

2. The one of the following that is LEAST useful to a clerk employed in the mail unit of a large city department is knowing the

    A. functions of the various divisions in the department
    B. names of the various division heads
    C. location of the various divisions
    D. salaries of the various division heads

3. A clerk notices that a visitor has just entered the office. The other clerks are not aware of the visitor's presence. The MOST appropriate of the following actions for the clerk to take is to

    A. attend to the visitor immediately
    B. continue with his own work and leave the handling of the visitor to one of the other clerks
    C. cough loudly to direct the attention of the other clerks to the presence of the visitor
    D. continue with his work unless the visitor addresses him directly

4. When a record is borrowed from the files, the file clerk puts a substitution or *out* card in its place.
    Of the following, the information that is LEAST commonly placed on the *out* card is

    A. who borrowed the record
    B. when the record was borrowed
    C. why the record was borrowed
    D. what record was borrowed

5. Of the following, the BEST method of maintaining a mailing list that is subject to frequent changes is to keep the names in a

    A. loose-leaf address book in which twenty names are entered on each page
    B. card file in which each name is entered on a separate card
    C. bound address book in which twenty-five names are entered on each page
    D. card file in which ten names are entered on each card

29

6. Of the following, the MAIN reason for using window envelopes instead of plain envelopes in mailing correspondence is that

   A. window envelopes cost less
   B. the address is less likely to be defaced during delivery
   C. addressing the envelopes is eliminated
   D. the postal rate for window envelopes is less

7. It is frequently helpful to file material under two subjects. In such a case, the material is filed under one subject and a card indicating where the material is filed is placed under the other subject.
   This card is known GENERALLY as a _____ card.

   A. follow-up or tickler   B. guide
   C. transfer   D. cross-reference

8. In taking down a telephone message for an employee who is absent from the office, a clerk should consider it LEAST important to indicate in his note to the absent employee the

   A. time the call was received
   B. number of the telephone extension on which the call came in
   C. name of the clerk who took the message
   D. caller's telephone number

9. A mail clerk whose supervisor has instructed him to send certain items by *parcel post* should send them by

   A. fourth-class mail   B. Railway Express
   C. registered first class mail   D. second-class mail

10. Of the following, the MOST appropriate greeting for a receptionist to use in addressing visitors is

    A. "Please state your business."
    B. "May I help you?"
    C. "Hello. What is your problem?"
    D. "Do you wish to see someone?"

11. A clerk assigned to the task of adding several long columns of figures performs this work on an adding machine that prints the figures on a paper tape.
    In general, the MOST efficient of the following methods of checking the accuracy of the computations is for the clerk to

    A. check the figures on the paper tape against the corresponding figures in the original material
    B. repeat the computations on the adding machine, using the figures appearing on the paper tape, and then check to see whether the totals on the two tapes are the same
    C. perform the computations manually and check the totals thus obtained against the totals obtained by machine operation
    D. have another clerk repeat the computations manually and check the totals obtained in these two sets of computations

12. The term *via* means MOST NEARLY

    A. by way of
    B. face to face
    C. return postage guaranteed
    D. value indicated above

13. A clerk assigned to open and sort incoming mail notices that an envelope does not contain the enclosure referred to in the letter.
    The MOST appropriate of the following actions for him to take is to

    A. delay the delivery of the letter for one day since the enclosure may turn up in the next day's mail
    B. forward the letter to the person to whom it is addressed with an indication that the enclosure was omitted
    C. forward the letter to the person to whom it is addressed and send a tracer inquiry to the post office
    D. return the letter to the writer with a request for the enclosure mentioned in the letter

14. To obtain MOST quickly the telephone number of the General Post Office in the telephone directory, one should look FIRST under the listing

    A. General Post Office
    B. Federal Government
    C. United States Government
    D. Post Office Department

15. While your supervisor is at lunch, a visitor approaches you and asks for information regarding an important matter. Although you have no information about the matter, you know that your supervisor has just received a confidential report on the subject and that the report is still in your supervisor's desk.
    The MOST appropriate of the following actions for you to take is to

    A. obtain the report from your supervisor's desk and permit the visitor to read it in your presence
    B. tell the visitor that your supervisor has just received a report on this matter and suggest that the visitor ask your supervisor for permission to read it
    C. inform the visitor that you have no information on the matter and suggest that he return later when the supervisor will be back from lunch
    D. obtain the report from your supervisor's desk and answer the visitor's questions from information contained in the report

16. The two sets of initials that are usually placed on the bottom of a business letter flush with the left-hand margin and on a line with the last line of the signature indicate

    A. where the letter should be filed
    B. who dictated the letter and who typed it
    C. which persons received copies of the letter
    D. how the letter should be routed

17. When payment of the personal check of a depositor is guaranteed by his bank, that check is called a

    A. bank draft
    B. voucher check
    C. cashier's check
    D. certified check

18. The *Ditto* machine is a(n) _____ machine.

    A. duplicating
    B. transcribing
    C. dictating
    D. adding

19. The classified telephone directory is known GENERALLY as The

   A. Consumers' Buying Guide
   B. Business Index
   C. Red Book
   D. Commodity Exchange

20. Department X employs 500 men who work in 20 different skilled trades. These men are paid at an hourly rate which differs for each skilled trade. They are paid weekly. The number of hours worked by a man varies from week to week. The timekeeping clerk computes the number of hours a week worked by each man, and the following devices that may be used each week to determine the weekly earnings of each of these 500 men, the one that will be MOST helpful to the payroll clerk, is a

   A. listing type of adding machine
   B. non-listing type of adding machine
   C. graph showing the average number of hours worked and the average hourly rate of pay for each week of the previous year
   D. table listing the amounts obtained by multiplying hourly rates of pay by number of hours worked

21. A cash fund kept on hand for the payment of minor office expenses is known GENERALLY as

   A. petty cash
   B. a sinking fund
   C. a drawing account
   D. net assets

22. The term that describes the connection between the inter-office computer technology is

   A. interface
   B. network
   C. hardware
   D. software

23. Complaints from the public are no longer regarded by government officials as mere nuisances. Instead, complaints are often welcomed because they frequently bring into the open conditions and faults in operation and service which should be corrected.
   This statement means MOST NEARLY that

   A. government officials now realize that complaints from the public are necessary
   B. faulty operations and services are not brought into the open except by complaints from the public
   C. government officials now realize that complaints from the public are in reality a sign of a well-run organization
   D. complaints from the public can be useful in indicating needs for improvement in operation and service

Questions 24-26.

DIRECTIONS: Questions 24 to 26 are to be answered SOLELY on the basis of the information contained in the following statement.

The most important unit of the mimeograph machine is a perforated metal drum over which is stretched a cloth ink pad. A reservoir inside the drum contains the ink which flows through the perforations and saturates the ink pad. To operate the machine, the operator first removes from the machine the protective sheet, which keeps the ink from drying while the machine is not in use. He then hooks the stencil face down on the drum, draws the stencil smoothly over the drum, and fastens the stencil at the bottom. The speed with which the drum turns determines the blackness of the copies printed. Slow turning gives heavy, black copies; fast turning gives light, clear-cut reproductions. If reproductions are run on other than porous paper, slip-sheeting is necessary to prevent smearing. Often the printed copy fails to drop readily as it comes from the machine. This may be due to static electricity. To remedy this difficulty, the operator fastens a strip of tinsel from side to side near the impression roller so that the printed copy just touches the soft stems of the tinsel as it is ejected from the machine, thus grounding the static electricity to the frame of the machine.

24. According to this statement, 24._____

    A. turning the drum fast produces light copies
    B. stencils should be placed face up on the drum
    C. ink pads should be changed daily
    D. slip-sheeting is necessary when porous paper is being used

25. According to this statement, when a mimeograph machine is not in use, the 25._____

    A. ink should be drained from the drum
    B. ink pad should be removed
    C. machine should be covered with a protective sheet
    D. counter should be set at zero

26. According to this statement, static electricity is grounded to the frame of the mimeograph machine by means of 26._____

    A. a slip-sheeting device
    B. a strip of tinsel
    C. an impression roller
    D. hooks located at the top of the drum

Questions 27-28.

DIRECTIONS: Questions 27 and 28 are to be answered SOLELY on the basis of the information contained in the following statement.

The proofreading of material typed from copy is performed more accurately and more speedily when two persons perform this work as a team. The person who did not do the typing should read aloud the original copy while the person who did the typing should check the reading against the typed copy. The reader should speak very slowly and repeat the figures, using a different grouping of numbers when repeating the figures. For example, in reading 1967, the reader may say 'one-nine-six-seven' on first reading the figure and 'nineteen-sixty-seven' on repeating the figure. The reader should read all punctuation marks, taking nothing for granted. Since mistakes can occur anywhere, everything typed should be proofread. To avoid confusion, the proofreading team should use the standard proofreading marks, which are given in most dictionaries.

27. According to this statement,

    A. the person who holds the typed copy is called the reader
    B. the two members of a proofreading team should take turns in reading the typed copy aloud
    C. the typed copy should be checked by the person who did the typing
    D. the person who did not do the typing should read aloud from the typed copy

28. According to this statement,

    A. it is unnecessary to read the period at the end of a sentence
    B. typographical errors should be noted on the original copy
    C. each person should develop his own set of proofreading marks
    D. figures should be read twice

29. When questioned by his supervisor, the clerk said, "*I have never begin a new assignment until I have completely finished whatever I am working on.*"
    This statement may BEST be characterized as

    A. *foolish;* work should be orderly
    B. *foolish;* every task must be completed sooner or later
    C. *wise;* unfinished work is an index of inefficiency
    D. *foolish;* some assignments should be undertaken immediately

30. Suppose that a clerk in your office has been transferred to another unit. After a brief period of training, you are assigned to his duties. An important problem arises, and you are uncertain as to the most advisable course of action.
    For you to telephone the clerk whose place you are taking and to ask his advice would be

    A. *wise;* his interest in your welfare will be stimulated
    B. *foolish;* incompetence is admitted
    C. *foolish;* learning is best accomplished by doing
    D. *wise;* useful guidance may be obtained

31. Suppose that a file cabinet, which has a capacity of 3,000 cards, now contains approximately 2,200 cards. Cards are added to the file at the average rate of 30 cards a day.
    To find the number of days it will take to fill the cabinet to capacity,

    A. divide 3,000 by 30
    B. divide 2,200 by 3,000
    C. divide 800 by 30
    D. multiply 30 by the fraction 2,200 divided by 3,000

32. A *tickler file* is used CHIEFLY for

    A. unsorted papers which the file clerk has not had time to file
    B. personnel records
    C. pending matters which should receive attention at some particular time
    D. index to cross-referenced material

33. A new file clerk who has not become thoroughly familiar with the files in unable to locate *McLeod* in the correspondence files under *Mo* and asks your help.
    Of the following, the BEST reply to give her is that

    A. there probably is no correspondence in the files for that person
    B. she probably has the name spelled wrong and should verify the spelling
    C. she will probably find the correspondence under *McLeod* as the files are arranged with the prefix *Mc* considered as *Mac* (as if the name were spelled *MacLeod*)
    D. the correspondence folder for *McLeod* has evidently been misplaced or borrowed from the files

34. If your superior asks you a question to which you do not know the answer, you should say

    A. "That is not my work."
    B. "I'm sorry, I do not know."
    C. "I do not know but you can look it up in the files."
    D. "Ask Miss Jones. I think she knows something about that matter."

35. Of the following, for which reason are cross-references necessary in filing?

    A. There is a choice of terms under which the correspondence may be filed.
    B. The only filing information contained in the correspondence is the name of the writer.
    C. Records are immediately visible without searching through the files.
    D. Persons other than file clerks can easily locate material.

36. The Federal Bureau of Investigation is a bureau in the Department of

    A. Justice   B. Defense   C. the Interior   D. State

37. A citizen of the United States who wishes to obtain a passport permitting him to visit a foreign country should apply at the office of the United States Department of

    A. Defense   B. Justice   C. the Interior   D. State

38. The permanent headquarters of the United Nations is in

    A. Geneva   B. Moscow   C. Paris   D. New York City

39. Six gross of special drawing pencils were purchased for use in a city department. If the pencils were used at the rate of 24 a week, the MAXIMUM number of weeks that the six gross of pencils would last is _____ weeks.

    A. 6   B. 12   C. 24   D. 36

40. A stock clerk had 600 pads on hand. He then issued 3/8 of his supply of pads to Division X, 1/4 to Division Y, and 1/6 to Division Z.
    The number of pads remaining in stock is

    A. 48   B. 125   C. 240   D. 475

41. If a certain job can be performed by 18 clerks in 26 days, the number of clerks needed to perform the job in 12 days is _____ clerks.

    A. 24   B. 30   C. 39   D. 52

Questions 42-50.

DIRECTIONS: Each of Questions 42 to 50 consists of four names. For each question, select the one of the four names that should be THIRD if the four names were arranged in alphabetical order in accordance with the Rules for Alphabetical Filing given below. For each question, print in the correspondingly numbered space at the right the letter preceding the name that should be THIRD in alphabetical order.

RULES FOR ALPHABETICAL FILING

NAMES OF INDIVIDUALS

(1) Names of individuals are to be filed in strict alphabetical order. This order is determined first according to the last name, then according to the first name or initial, and finally according to the middle name or initial (if any).

(2) Where two last names are identical, the one with an initial instead of a first name precedes the one with a first name that begins with the same initial letter. For example: Cole precedes Edward Cole.

(3) Where two last names are identical and the two first names are also identical, the one without a middle name or initial precedes the one with a middle name or initial. For example: Edward Cole precedes both Edward R. Cole and Edward Robert Cole.

(4) Where two last names are identical and the two first names are also identical, the one with a middle initial precedes the one with a middle name beginning with the same initial letter.
For example: Edward R. Cole precedes Edward Robert Cole.

(5) Prefixes such as D', De, La, Le, Mac, Mc, O', and von are considered parts of the names they precede. These names should be filed as spelled. For example: Peter La Farge precedes John Le Blanc.

(6) Treat all abbreviations as if spelled out in full when the names for which they stand are commonly understood.

NAMES OF BUSINESS ORGANIZATIONS

(1) Names of business organizations are filed in alphabetical order as written, except that a name containing the name of an individual is filed in accordance with the rules given for filing names of individuals. For example: John Cole Varnish Co. precedes Federal Trust Co.

(2) Names composed of numerals or abbreviations are to be treated as though the numerals or abbreviations were spelled out.

(3) Disregard the following in alphabetizing: and, the, of.

SAMPLE:
- (A) Adam Dunn (2)
- (B) E. Dunn (3)
- (C) A. Duncan (1)
- (D) Edward Robert Dunn (4)

The numbers in parentheses indicate the proper alphabetical order in which these names should be filed. Since the name that should be filed THIRD is E. Dunn, the answer is B.

42. A. William Carver B. Howard Cambell
    C. Arthur Chambers D. Charles Banner
    42.____

43. A. Paul Moore B. William Moore
    C. Paul A. Moore D. William Allen Moore
    43.____

44. A. George Peters B. Eric Petersen
    C. G. Peters D. Petersen
    44.____

45. A. Edward Hallam B. Jos. Frank Hamilton
    C. Edward A. Hallam D. Joseph F. Hamilton
    45.____

46. A. Theodore Madison B. Timothy McGill
    C. Thomas MacLane D. Thomas A. Madison
    46.____

47. A. William O'Hara B. Arthur Gordon
    C. James DeGraff D. Anne von Glatin
    47.____

48. A. Charles Green B. Chas. T. Greene
    C. Charles Thomas Greene D. Wm. A. Greene
    48.____

49. A. John Foss Insurance Co. B. New World Stove Co.
    C. 14th Street Dress Shop D. Arthur Stein Paper Co.
    49.____

50. A. Gold Trucking Co. B. 8th Ave. Garage
    C. The First National Bank D. The Century Novelty Co.
    50.____

KEY (CORRECT ANSWERS)

1. C	11. A	21. A	31. C	41. C
2. D	12. A	22. B	32. C	42. A
3. A	13. B	23. D	33. C	43. B
4. C	14. C	24. A	34. B	44. D
5. B	15. C	25. C	35. A	45. D
6. C	16. B	26. B	36. A	46. D
7. D	17. D	27. C	37. D	47. A
8. B	18. A	28. D	38. D	48. C
9. A	19. C	29. C	39. D	49. B
10. B	20. D	30. C	40. B	50. C

TEST 2

DIRECTIONS: Each question or incomplete statement is followed by several suggested answers or completions. Select the one that BEST answers the question or completes the statement. *PRINT THE LETTER OF THE CORRECT ANSWER IN THE SPACE AT THE RIGHT.*

1. *The supervisor's instructions were terse*. The word *terse* as used in this sentence means MOST NEARLY

    A. detailed B. harsh C. vague D. concise

2. *He did not wish to evade these issues.* The word *evade* as used in this sentence means MOST NEARLY

    A. avoid B. examine C. settle D. discuss

3. *The prospects for an early settlement were dubious.* The word *dubious* as used in this sentence means MOST NEARLY

    A. strengthened B. uncertain C. weakened D. cheerful

4. *The visitor was morose.* The word *morose* as used in this sentence means MOST NEARLY

    A. curious B. gloomy C. impatient D. timid

5. *He was unwilling to impede the work of his unit.* The word *impede* as used in this sentence means MOST NEARLY

    A. carry out B. criticize C. praise D. hinder

6. *The remuneration was unsatisfactory.* The word *remuneration* as used in this sentence means MOST NEARLY

    A. payment B. summary C. explanation D. estimate

7. A *recurring* problem is one that

    A. replaces a problem that existed previously
    B. is unexpected
    C. has long been overlooked
    D. comes up from time to time

8. *His subordinates were aware of this magnanimous act.* The word *magnanimous* as used in this sentence means MOST NEARLY

    A. insolent B. shrewd C. unselfish D. threatening

9. *The new employee is a zealous worker.* The word *zealous* as used in this sentence means MOST NEARLY

    A. awkward B. untrustworthy
    C. enthusiastic D. skillful

10. To *impair* means MOST NEARLY to

    A. weaken B. conceal C. improve D. expose

11. *The unit head was in a quandary.* The word *quandary* as used in this sentence means MOST NEARLY

    A. violent dispute
    B. puzzling predicament
    C. angry mood
    D. strong position

12. *His actions were judicious.* The word *judicious* as used in this sentence means MOST NEARLY

    A. wise   B. biased   C. final   D. limited

13. *His report contained many irrelevant statements.* The word *irrelevant* as used in this sentence means MOST NEARLY

    A. unproven
    B. not pertinent
    C. hard to understand
    D. insincere

14. *He was not present at the inception of the program.* The word *inception* as used in this sentence means MOST NEARLY

    A. beginning   B. discussion   C. conclusion   D. rejection

15. The word *solicitude* means MOST NEARLY

    A. request   B. isolation   C. seriousness   D. concern

Questions 16-30.

DIRECTIONS: Each of the sentences numbered 16 to 30 may be classified MOST appropriately under one of the following four categories:
A. faulty because of incorrect grammar or word usage
B. faulty because of incorrect punctuation
C. faulty because of incorrect capitalization
D. correct

Examine each sentence carefully. Then, in the correspondingly numbered space at the right, print the letter preceding the option which is the BEST of the four suggested above. All incorrect sentences contain but one type of error. Consider a sentence correct if it contains none of the types of errors mentioned, even though there may be other correct ways of expressing the same thought.

16. He was not informed, that he would have to work overtime.

17. The wind blew several papers off of his desk.

18. Charles Dole, who is a member of the committee, was asked to confer with commissioner Wilson.

19. Miss Bell will issue a copy to whomever asks for one.

20. Most employees, and he is no exception do not like to work overtime.

21. This is the man whom you interviewed last week. 21.____
22. Of the two cities visited, White Plains is the cleanest. 22.____
23. Although he was willing to work on other holidays, he refused to work on Labor day. 23.____
24. If an employee wishes to attend the conference, he should fill out the necessary forms. 24.____
25. The division chief reports that an engineer and an inspector is needed for this special survey. 25.____
26. The work was assigned to Miss Green and me. 26.____
27. The staff regulations state that an employee, who is frequently tardy, may receive a negative evaluation. 27.____
28. He is the kind of person who is always willing to undertake difficult assignments. 28.____
29. Mr. Wright's request cannot be granted under no conditions. 29.____
30. George Colt a new employee, was asked to deliver the report to the Domestic Relations Court. 30.____

Questions 31-40.

DIRECTIONS: Each of Questions 31 to 40 consists of four words. One of the words in each question is spelled INCORRECTLY. For each question, print in the correspondingly numbered space at the right the letter preceding the word which is INCORRECTLY spelled.

31.	A. primery	B. mechanic	C. referred	D. admissible	31.____
32.	A. cessation	B. beleif	C. aggressive	D. allowance	32.____
33.	A. leisure	B. authentic	C. familiar	D. contemptable	33.____
34.	A. volume	B. forty	C. dilemma	D. seldum	34.____
35.	A. discrepancy	B. aquisition	C. exorbitant	D. lenient	35.____
36.	A. simultanous	B. penetrate	C. revision	D. conspicuous	36.____
37.	A. ilegible	B. gracious	C. profitable	D. obedience	37.____
38.	A. manufacturer	B. authorize	C. compelling	D. peculiar	38.____
39.	A. anxious	B. rehearsal	C. handicaped	D. tendency	39.____
40.	A. meticulous	B. accompaning	C. initiative	D. shelves	40.____

Questions 41-50.

DIRECTIONS: Questions 41 to 50 are based on the Personnel Record of Division X shown below. Refer to this table when answering these questions.

DIVISION X
PERSONNEL RECORD - CURRENT YEAR

Employee	Bureau in Which Employed	Title	Annual Salary	No. of Days Absent On Vacation	No. of Days Absent On Sick Leave	No. of Times Late
Abbott	Mail Bureau	Clerk	$31,200	18	0	1
Barnes	,,	Clerk	25,200	25	3	7
Davis	,,	Typist	24,000	21	9	2
Adams	Payroll Bureau	Accountant	42,500	10	0	2
Bell	,,	Bookkeeper	31,200	23	2	5
Duke	,,	Clerk	27,600	24	4	3
Gross	,,	Clerk	21,600	12	5	7
Lane	,,	Stenographer	26,400	19	16	20
Reed	,,	Typist	22,800	15	11	11
Arnold	Record Bureau	Clerk	32,400	6	15	9
Cane	,,	Clerk	24,500	14	3	4
Fay	,,	Clerk	21,100	20	0	4
Hale	,,	Typist	25,200	18	2	7
Baker	Supply Bureau	Clerk	30,000	20	3	2
Clark	,,	Clerk	27,600	25	6	5
Ford	,,	Typist	22,800	25	4	22

41. The percentage of the total number of employees who are clerks is MOST NEARLY

   A. 25%   B. 33%   C. 38%   D. 56%

42. Of the following employees, the one who receives a monthly salary of $2,100 is

   A. Barnes   B. Gross   C. Reed   D. Clark

43. The difference between the annual salary of the highest paid clerk and that of the lowest paid clerk is

   A. $6,000   B. $8,400   C. $11,300   D. $20,900

44. The number of employees receiving more than $25,000 a year but less than $40,000 a year is

   A. 6   B. 9   C. 12   D. 15

45. The total annual salary of the employees of the Mail Bureau is

   A. one-half of the total annual salary of the employees of the Payroll Bureau
   B. less than the total annual salary of the employees of the Record Bureau by $21,600
   C. equal to the total annual salary of the employees of the Supply Bureau
   D. less than the total annual salary of the employees of the Payroll Bureau by $71,600

46. The average annual salary of the employees who are NOT clerks is MOST NEARLY

   A. $23,700   B. $25,450   C. $26,800   D. $27,850

47. If all the employees were given a 10% increase in pay, the annual salary of Lane would then be 47.____

    A. greater than that of Barnes by $1,320
    B. less than that of Bell by $4,280
    C. equal to that of Clark
    D. greater than that of Ford by $3,600

48. Of the clerks who earned less than $30,000 a year, the one who was late the FEWEST number of times was late _____ time(s). 48.____

    A. 1 B. 2 C. 3 D. 4

49. The bureau in which the employees were late the FEWEST number of times on an average is the _____ Bureau. 49.____

    A. Mail B. Payroll C. Record D. Supply

50. The MOST accurate of the following statements is that 50.____

    A. Reed was late more often than any other typist
    B. Bell took more time off for vacation than any other employee earning $30,000 or more annually
    C. of the typists, Ford was the one who was absent the fewest number of times because of sickness
    D. three clerks took no time off because of sickness

KEY (CORRECT ANSWERS)

1. D	11. B	21. D	31. A	41. D
2. A	12. A	22. A	32. B	42. A
3. B	13. B	23. C	33. D	43. C
4. B	14. A	24. D	34. D	44. B
5. D	15. D	25. A	35. B	45. C
6. A	16. B	26. D	36. A	46. D
7. D	17. A	27. B	37. A	47. A
8. C	18. C	28. D	38. D	48. C
9. C	19. A	29. A	39. C	49. A
10. A	20. B	30. B	40. B	50. B

EXAMINATION SECTION
TEST 1

DIRECTIONS: Each question or incomplete statement is followed by several suggested answers or completions. Select the one that BEST answers the question or completes the statement. *PRINT THE LETTER OF THE CORRECT ANSWER IN THE SPACE AT THE RIGHT.*

1. A city agency whose employees come into frequent contact with the public can gain public approval of its work MOST effectively by 1.____

    A. distributing pamphlets describing its objectives and work to the people who come into contact with the agency
    B. encouraging its employees to behave properly when off duty so as to impress the public favorably
    C. making certain that its employees perform their daily services efficiently and courteously
    D. having its officials give lectures to civic groups, describing the agency's efficiency and accomplishments

2. Assume that you are a newly appointed clerk in a city agency. While your superior is at a conference that may last for several hours, a visitor enters the office and asks you for information on certain of your agency's procedures with which you are not familiar.
Of the following, the BEST action for you to take is to 2.____

    A. ask the visitor to return to the office later in the day when your superior will have returned
    B. ask the visitor to wait in the office until your superior returns
    C. ask a more experienced clerk in your office to answer the visitor's questions
    D. advise the visitor that the information that he is seeking will be given to him if he writes to your superior

3. A visitor to an office in a city agency tells one of the clerks that he has an appointment with the supervisor of the office who is expected shortly. The visitor asks for permission to wait in the supervisor's private office, which is unoccupied at the moment.
For the clerk to allow the visitor to do so would be 3.____

    A. *desirable;* the visitor would be less likely to disturb the other employees or to be disturbed by them
    B. *undesirable;* it is not courteous to permit a visitor to be left alone in an office
    C. *desirable;* the supervisor may wish to speak to the visitor in private
    D. *undesirable;* the supervisor may have left confidential papers on his desk

4. Mr. Jones is a clerk in Bureau A in a city agency. Of the following, the MOST appropriate statement for Mr. Jones to make when answering the telephone in his office is 4.____

    A. "Hello. This is Mr. Jones."
    B. "Bureau A, Mr. Jones."
    C. "This is Bureau A. What can we do for you?"
    D. "Bureau A, who is this please?"

5. Your supervisor has given you about two thousand 3x5 cards to arrange in alphabetical order.
   For you first to sort the cards into several broad groups, such as A to E, F to K, etc., and then alphabetize each group of cards separately is

   A. *desirable;* proportionately less time is required to sort small groups of cards than large groups of cards
   B. *undesirable;* a process of alphabetizing which requires more than one step wastes too much time
   C. *desirable;* full use can then be made of all information on the cards
   D. *undesirable;* fewer alphabetizing errors will be made in a small group of cards than in a large group of cards

6. A clerk assigned to the mail unit of a city agency has completed his assigned duties for the day about two hours before closing time.
   In this situation, it is MOST advisable for the clerk to

   A. do some of his work over again in order to attain greater skill
   B. report to his supervisor that he has completed his assignment
   C. ask the supervisor of an adjoining unit for permission to observe the work of that unit
   D. ask a fellow employee if he would like to have help in completing his work for the day

7. A mail clerk assigned to the task of inserting outgoing letters into envelopes notices that one letter has not been signed.
   The MOST appropriate of the following actions for the clerk to take is to

   A. sign the letter with his own name
   B. sign the letter with the dictator's name and his own initials
   C. return the letter to the dictator for signature
   D. mail the letter without the signature

8. The MOST important characteristic of a tickler card file is that the cards are arranged according to

   A. subject matter
   B. the date on which action is to be taken
   C. the name of the individual on the card
   D. the order of importance of the items contained on the cards

9. As a clerk in a city department, one of your duties is to maintain the files in your bureau. Material from these files is sometimes used by other bureaus. You frequently find that you are unable to locate some material because it has been removed from the files and is evidently being used by some other bureau.
   The BEST way to correct this situation is to

   A. have an out-of-file card filled out and filed whenever material is borrowed from the files
   B. forbid employees of other bureaus to borrow material from the files unless they promise to return it promptly
   C. provide other bureaus with duplicate files
   D. notify your supervisor whenever an employee from another bureau is slow in returning material to the files

10. Assume that you are assigned as stock room clerk in your department. 10.____
Of the following practices, the one that would be LEAST advisable for you to follow is that

   A. the supply of an article should be exhausted before a new supply is ordered
   B. articles requested frequently should be stored in a readily available place
   C. units of an article should, in general, be stored so that the oldest is used first
   D. articles should not be issued without a requisition slip

11. The Post Office prefers that all outgoing addresses be typewritten or in ink, rather than in pencil. 11.____
Of the following, the BEST reason for this preference is that

   A. a pencil address may smudge and become illegible
   B. an address which is typewritten or written in ink is neater
   C. the addressee may wish to retain the envelope for his records
   D. unauthorized changes of addresses are discouraged

12. A city agency that has recently moved to a new address has started a campaign to reduce the wasteful use of supplies. There are on hand about three thousand legal-sized envelopes bearing the old return address. 12.____
In view of this conservation policy, the MOST appropriate action to take with the envelopes would be to

   A. send them only to people who know the new address
   B. use them to store small items like clips and rubber bands
   C. use them only for first class mail
   D. block out the old address and stamp in the new one

13. The abbreviation *Enc.* which sometimes appears on a business letter flush with the left-hand margin and one 13.____
or two lines below the line of the signature indicates that

   A. a carbon copy of the letter has been prepared
   B. a prompt reply to the letter is expected
   C. no reply to the letter is necessary
   D. other papers accompany the letter

14. Assume that you have been instructed to prepare a copy of a statistical table describing your bureau's activities. The BEST method for making certain that no error has been made in preparing the copy is for you to 14.____

   A. compare all the totals and subtotals in the two tables, for if they are identical on the two tables, the copy may be assumed to be accurate
   B. spot check the places in the two tables where errors are most likely to occur
   C. have another clerk read the original table aloud to you while you check the copy
   D. request another clerk to prepare a second copy independently and then compare the two copies

15. A transfer file is used PRIMARILY to 15.____

    A. carry records from one office to another
    B. store inactive records
    C. hold records that are constantly used by more than one bureau of an organization
    D. hold confidential records

16. The usual reason for endorsement of a check is to 16.____

    A. transfer ownership of the check
    B. identify the drawer of the check
    C. indicate that the check is genuine
    D. prevent payment of the check until a specific date

17. An estimate of revenues and expenditures for the next fiscal year prepared by a governmental organization or a private firm is called a(n) 17.____

    A. budget   B. appropriation   C. voucher   D. inventory

18. It is required that a clerk satisfactorily complete a probationary period before his appointment to a city job is considered permanent. 18.____
    Of the following, the BEST reason for this requirement is that

    A. success on one job is a good indication of success in the next higher job
    B. a clerk usually performs his work more efficiently during his probationary period than after that period is completed
    C. actual performance on a job is the most valid test of a clerk's ability to do the work
    D. the rating a person receives on a civil service examination is usually just as significant as the efficiency he demonstrates during his probationary period

19. A government agency should have an established practice of disposing of papers, correspondence, and records that are no longer of any use. 19.____
    Of the following, the LEAST important reason for establishing such a practice is the necessity of

    A. conserving space whenever possible
    B. saving time in filing and locating papers
    C. releasing filing equipment for current needs
    D. obtaining income from the sale of the waste paper

20. Since the government can spend only what it obtains from the people and this amount is ultimately limited by their capacity and willingness to pay taxes, it is very important that they should be given full information about the work of the government. 20.____
    According to this statement,

    A. governmental employees should be trained not only in their own work, but also in how to perform the duties of other employees in their agency
    B. taxation by the government rests upon the consent of the people
    C. the release of full information on the work of the government will increase the efficiency of governmental operations
    D. the work of the government, in recent years, has been restricted because of reduced tax collections

Questions 21-23.

DIRECTIONS: Questions 21 to 23 are to be answered SOLELY on the information contained in the following statement.

The equipment in a mail room may include a mail metering machine. This machine simultaneously stamps, postmarks, seals, and counts letters as fast as the operator can feed them. It can also print the proper postage directly on a gummed strip to be affixed to bulky items. It is equipped with a meter which is removed from the machine and sent to the postmaster to be set for a given number of stampings of any denomination. The setting of the meter must be paid for in advance. One of the advantages of metered mail is that it bypasses the cancellation operation and thereby facilitates handling by the post office. Mail metering also makes the pilfering of stamps impossible, but does not prevent the passage of personal mail in company envelopes through the meters unless there is established a rigid control or censorship over outgoing mail.

21. According to this statement, the postmaster   21._____
    A. is responsible for training new clerks in the use of mail metering machines
    B. usually recommends that both large and small firms adopt the use of mail metering machines
    C. is responsible for setting the meter to print a fixed number of stampings
    D. examines the mail metering machines to see that they are properly installed in the mail room

22. According to this statement, the use of mail metering machines   22._____
    A. requires the employment of more clerks in a mail room than does the use of postage stamps
    B. interferes with the handling of large quantities of outgoing mail
    C. does not prevent employees from sending their personal letters at company expense
    D. usually involves smaller expenditures for mail room equipment than does the use of postage stamps

23. On the basis of this statement, it is MOST accurate to state that   23._____
    A. mail metering machines are often used for opening envelopes
    B. postage stamps are generally used when bulky packages are to be mailed
    C. the use of metered mail tends to interfere with rapid mail handling by the post office
    D. mail metering machines can seal and count letters at the same time

Questions 24-25.

DIRECTIONS: Questions 24 and 25 are to be answered SOLELY on the basis of the information contained in the following statement.

Forms are printed sheets of paper on which information is to be entered. While what is printed on the form is most important, the kind of paper used in making the form is also important. The kind of paper should be selected with regard to the use to which the form will be subjected. Printing a form on an unnecessarily expensive grade of papers is wasteful. On the other hand, using too cheap or flimsy a form can materially interfere with satisfactory performance of the work the form is being planned to do. Thus, a form printed on both sides normally requires a heavier paper than a form printed only on one side. Forms to be used as permanent records, or which are expected to have a very long life in files, require a quality of paper which will not disintegrate or discolor with age. A form which will go through a great deal of handling requires a strong tough paper, while thinness is a necessary qualification where the making of several copies of a form will be required.

24. According to this statement, the type of paper used for making forms

    A. should be chosen in accordance with the use to which the form will be put
    B. should be chosen before the type of printing to be used has been decided upon
    C. is as important as the information which is printed on it
    D. should be strong enough to be used for any purpose

25. According to this statement, forms that are

    A. printed on both sides are usually economical and desirable
    B. to be filed permanently should not deteriorate as time goes on
    C. expected to last for a long time should be handled carefully
    D. to be filed should not be printed on inexpensive paper

26. The CHIEF purpose of assessing real estate each year is to determine

    A. the amount of real estate tax that the owner must pay
    B. the value of unused real estate in the city
    C. the improvements that the owner must make in his property
    D. how the property is being used

27. Certain types of local laws are submitted to the voters for approval. The submission of these laws to the voters for approval is known as

    A. the initiative   B. proportional representation
    C. the referendum   D. eminent domain

28. A new alphabetical name card file covering fifteen file drawers has been set up in your office. Your supervisor asks you to place identifying labels outside each file drawer.
    Of the following, the BEST rule for you to follow in determining the appropriate label for each drawer is that

    A. the alphabet should be divided equally among the file drawers available
    B. each label should give the beginning and ending points of the cards in that drawer
    C. each drawer should begin with a new letter of the alphabet
    D. no drawer should contain more than two letters of the alphabet

29. One of the administrators in your department cannot find an important letter left on his desk. He believes that the letter may accidentally have been placed among a group of letters sent to you for filing. You look in the file and find the letter filed in its correct place.
    Of the following, the BEST suggestion for you to make to your supervisor in order to avoid repetition of such incidents is that

    A. file clerks should be permitted to read material they are requested to file
    B. correspondence files should be cross-indexed
    C. a periodic check should be made of the files to locate material inaccurately filed
    D. material which is sent to the file clerk should be marked *O.K. for filing*

30. One of your duties is to keep a file of administrative orders by date. Your supervisor often asks you to find the order concerning a particular subject. Since you are rarely able to remember the date of the order, it is necessary for you to search through the entire file. Of the following, the BEST suggestion for you to make to your supervisor for remedying this situation is that

    A. each order bear conspicuously in its upper left-hand corner the precise date on which it is issued
    B. old orders be taken from the file and destroyed as soon as they are superseded by new orders, so that the file will not be overcrowded
    C. an alphabetic subject index of orders be prepared so that orders can be located easily by content as well as date
    D. dates be eliminated entirely from orders

31. Suppose that a fixed number of entries must be made on record cards each month. Because of military leaves, the number of clerks assigned to this work has been reduced by 20 percent over last year, although the total number of entries made remains the same.
    Of the following, the MOST accurate statement is that, as compared with last year, the average number of entries now made by each clerk has

    A. remained the same
    B. increased 20 percent
    C. decreased 20 percent
    D. increased 25 percent

32. Suppose that the employees in your department are classified in five age groups. Your supervisor asks you to find the percentage of employees in each of the five age groups. Of the following, the BEST method to employ for checking the accuracy of your arithmetic in computing the percentages is to

    A. arrange the five percentages in increasing order of magnitude
    B. reduce the five percentages to common terms
    C. add the five percentages
    D. divide each percentage by the total number of individuals in that age group

33. Suppose that you are newly assigned to a large office in your department. You believe that a certain change in office routine would be desirable.
    Of the following, the BEST reason for suggesting this modification to your supervisor is that

    A. even good supervisors are sometimes reluctant to institute innovations
    B. your suggestion may result in the saving of considerable time and money
    C. major changes in office routine are easier to make in small offices than in large offices
    D. a new employee will usually be able to think of new ways of doing his work

34. A clerk divided his 35-hour work week as follows:
    1/5 of his time in sorting mail;
    1/2 of his time in filing letters; and
    1/7 of his time in reception work.
    The rest of his time was devoted to messenger work. The percentage of time spent on messenger work by the clerk during the week was MOST NEARLY

    A. 6% B. 10% C. 14% D. 16%

35. A city department has set up a computing unit and has rented 5 computing machines at a monthly rental of $140 per machine. In addition, the cost to the department for the maintenance and repair of each of these machines is $10 per month. Five computing machine operators, each receiving a monthly salary of $3,000, and a supervisor, who receives $3,800 a month, have been assigned to this unit. This unit will perform the work previously performed by 10 employees whose combined salary was $32,400 a month. On the basis of these facts, the savings that will result from the operation of this computing unit for 5 months will be MOST NEARLY

   A. $50,000   B. $64,000   C. $66,000   D. $95,000

36. Twelve clerks are assigned to enter certain data on index cards. This number of clerks could perform the task in 18 days. After these clerks have worked on this assignment for 6 days, 4 more clerks are added to the staff to do this work.
   Assuming that all the clerks work at the same rate of speed, the entire task, instead of taking 18 days, will be performed in _____ days.

   A. 9   B. 12   C. 15   D. 16

Questions 37-50.

DIRECTIONS: Each of Questions 37 to 50 consists of a word in capitals followed by four suggested meanings of the word. Print in the correspondingly numbered space at the right the letter preceding the word which means MOST NEARLY the same as the word in capitals.

37. FUNDAMENTAL
   A. adequate   B. essential   C. official   D. truthful

38. SUPPLANT
   A. approve   B. displace   C. satisfy   D. vary

39. OBLITERATE
   A. erase   B. demonstrate   C. review   D. detect

40. ANTICIPATE
   A. foresee   B. approve   C. annul   D. conceal

41. EXORBITANT
   A. priceless   B. extensive   C. worthless   D. excessive

42. RELUCTANT
   A. anxious   B. constant   C. drastic   D. hesitant

43. PREVALENT
   A. current   B. permanent   C. durable   D. temporary

44. AUGMENT
   A. conclude   B. suggest   C. increase   D. unite

45. FRUGAL   45.____
    A. friendly   B. thoughtful   C. hostile   D. economica
46. AUSTERITY   46.____
    A. priority   B. severity   C. anxiety   D. solitude
47. CORROBORATION   47.____
    A. expenditure   B. compilation   C. confirmation   D. reduction
48. IMPERATIVE   48.____
    A. impending   B. impossible   C. compulsory   D. logical
49. FEASIBLE   49.____
    A. simple   B. practicable   C. visible   D. lenient
50. SALUTARY   50.____
    A. popular   B. urgent   C. beneficial   D. forceful

KEY (CORRECT ANSWER)

1. C	11. A	21. C	31. D	41. D
2. C	12. D	22. C	32. C	42. D
3. D	13. D	23. D	33. B	43. A
4. B	14. C	24. A	34. D	44. C
5. A	15. B	25. B	35. B	45. D
6. B	16. A	26. A	36. C	46. B
7. C	17. A	27. C	37. B	47. C
8. B	18. C	28. B	38. B	48. C
9. A	19. D	29. B	39. A	49. B
10. A	20. B	30. C	40. A	50. C

TEST 2

DIRECTIONS: Each of Questions 1 to 2 consists of a word in capitals followed by four suggested meanings of the word. Print in the correspondingly numbered space at the right the letter preceding the word which means MOST NEARLY the same as the word in capitals.

1. ACQUIESCE 1.____
   A. endeavor   B. discharge   C. agree   D. inquire

2. DIFFIDENCE 2.____
   A. shyness   B. distinction   C. interval   D. discordance

Questions 3-17.

DIRECTIONS: Each of Questions 3 to 17 consists of a sentence which may be classified appropriately under one of the following four categories:
   A. incorrect because of faulty grammar or sentence structure
   B. incorrect because of faulty punctuation
   C. incorrect because of faulty capitalization
   D. correct

Examine each sentence carefully. Then, in the correspondingly numbered space at the right, print the letter preceding the option which is the BEST of the four suggested above. All incorrect sentences contain only one type of error. Consider a sentence correct if it contains none of the types of errors mentioned, although there may be other correct ways of expressing the same thought.

3. Mrs. Black the supervisor of the unit, has many important duties. 3.____

4. We spoke to the man whom you saw yesterday. 4.____

5. When a holiday falls on Sunday, it is officially celebrated on monday. 5.____

6. Of the two reports submitted, this one is the best. 6.____

7. Each staff member, including the accountants, were invited to the meeting. 7.____

8. Give the package to whomever calls for it. 8.____

9. To plan the work is our responsibility; to carry it out is his. 9.____

10. "May I see the person in charge of this office," asked the visitor? 10.____

11. He knows that it was not us who prepared the report. 11.____

12. These problems were brought to the attention of senator Johnson. 12.____

13. The librarian classifies all books periodicals and documents. 13.____

14. Any employee who uses an adding machine realizes its importance. 14.____

15. Instead of coming to the office, the clerk should of come to the supply room. 15.____

16. He asked, "will your staff assist us?" 16.____

17. Having been posted on the bulletin board, we were certain that the announcements would be read. 17.____

Questions 18-27.

DIRECTIONS: Each of Questions 18 to 27 consists of a group of four words. One word in each group is INCORRECTLY spelled. For each question, print in the correspondingly numbered space at the right the letter preceding the word which is INCORRECTLY spelled.

18.	A.	typical	B.	descend	C.	summarize	D.	continuel	18.____
19.	A.	courageous	B.	recomend	C.	omission	D.	eliminate	19.____
20.	A.	compliment	B.	illuminate	C.	auxilary	D.	installation	20.____
21.	A.	preliminary	B.	aquainted	C.	syllable	D.	analysis	21.____
22.	A.	accustomed	B.	negligible	C.	interupted	D.	bulletin	22.____
23.	A.	summoned	B.	managment	C.	mechanism	D.	sequence	23.____
24.	A.	commitee	B.	surprise	C.	noticeable	D.	emphasize	24.____
25.	A.	occurrance	B.	likely	C.	accumulate	D.	grievance	25.____
26.	A.	obstacle	B.	particuliar	C.	baggage	D.	fascinating	26.____
27.	A.	innumerable	B.	seize	C.	applicant	D.	dictionery	27.____

Questions 28-37.

DIRECTIONS: Each of Questions 28 to 37 consists of four names grouped vertically under four different filing arrangements lettered A, B, C, and D. In each question, only one of the four arrangements lists the names in the correct filing order according to the Rules for Alphabetical Filing given below. Read these rules carefully. Then, for each question, select the CORRECT filing arrangement, lettered A, B, C, or D and print in the appropriately numbered space at the right the letter of that CORRECT filing arrangement.

RULES FOR ALPHABETICAL FILING

NAMES OF INDIVIDUALS

(1) File all names of individuals in strict alphabetical order, first according to the last name, then according to first name or initial, and finally according to middle name or initial. For example: Robert Stone precedes Arnold Taft, and Edward H. Stone precedes G.A. Stone.

(2) Where the last names are identical, the one with an initial instead of a first name precedes the one with a first name beginning with the same initial. For example: R. Stone and R.B. Stone precede Robert Stone.

(3) Where two identical last names also have identical first names or initials, the one without a middle name or initial precedes the one with a middle name or initial. For example: R. Stone precedes R.B. Stone, and Robert Stone precedes Robert B. Stone.

(4) Where two identical last names also have identical first names or initials, the one with an initial instead of a middle name precedes the one with a middle name beginning with the same initial. For example: Robert B. Stone precedes Robert Burton Stone.

(5) Prefixes such as De, La, Le, and O' are considered as part of the names they precede. For example: John De Solle precedes Arthur Dexter.

(6) Names beginning with "Mac" and "Mc" are to be filed as spelled.

(7) Abbreviated names are to be treated as if they were spelled out. For example: Chas. stands for Charles, and Wm. stands for William.

(8) Titles and designations such as Dr., Mr., and Prof. are to be disregarded in filing.

NAMES OF BUSINESS ORGANIZATIONS

(1) File names of business organizations exactly as written, except that an organization bearing the name of an individual is filed alphabetically according to the name of the individual with the rules for filing names of individuals given above. For example: Thomas Miller Paper Co. precedes National Lumber Co.

(2) Where numerals occur in a name, they are to be treated as if they were spelled out. For example: 4 stands for four, and 8th stands for eighth.

(3) Where the following words occur in names, they are to be disregarded: the, of, and.

SAMPLE:

ARRANGEMENT A	ARRANGEMENT B	ARRANGEMENT C	ARRANGEMENT D
Arnold Robinson	Arthur Roberts	Arnold Robinson	Arthur Roberts
Arthur Roberts	J.B. Robin	Arthur Roberts	James Robin
J.B. Robin	James Robin	James Robin	J.B. Robin
James Robin	Arnold Robinson	J.B. Robin	Arnold Robinson

Since, in this sample, ARRANGEMENT B is the only one in which the four names are correctly arranged alphabetically, the answer is B.

28. ARRANGEMENT A   ARRANGEMENT B   28.___
     Alice Thompson   Eugene Thompkins
     Arnold G. Thomas   Alice Thompson
     B. Thomas   Arnold G. Thomas
     Eugene Thompkins   B. Thomas

4 (#2)

    ARRANGEMENT C
    B. Thomas
    Arnold G. Thomas
    Eugene Thompkins
    Alice Thompson

    ARRANGEMENT D
    Arnold G. Thomas
    B. Thomas
    Eugene Thompkins
    Alice Thompson

29. ARRANGEMENT A
    Albert Green
    A.B. Green
    Frank E. Green
    Wm. Greenfield

    ARRANGEMENT B
    A.B. Green
    Albert Green
    Frank E. Green
    Wm. Greenfield

29.____

    ARRANGEMENT C
    Albert Green
    Wm. Greenfield
    A.B. Green
    Frank E. Green

    ARRANGEMENT D
    A.B. Green
    Frank E. Green
    Albert Green
    Wm. Greenfield

30. ARRANGEMENT A
    Steven M. Comte
    Robt. Count
    Robert B. Count
    Steven Le Comte

    ARRANGEMENT B
    Steven Le Comte
    Steven M. Comte
    Robert B. Count
    Robt. Count

30.____

    ARRANGEMENT C
    Steven M. Comte
    Steven Le Comte
    Robt. Count
    Robert B. Count

    ARRANGEMENT D
    Robt. Count
    Robert B. Count
    Steven Le Comte
    Steven M. Comte

31. ARRANGEMENT A
    Prof. David Towner
    Miss Edna Tower
    Dr. Frank I. Tower
    Mrs. K.C. Towner

    ARRANGEMENT B
    Dr. Frank I. Tower
    Miss Edna Tower
    Mrs. K.C. Towner
    Prof. David Towner

31.____

    ARRANGEMENT C
    Miss Edna Tower
    Dr. Frank I. Tower
    Prof. David Towner
    Mrs. K.C. Towner

    ARRANGEMENT D
    Prof. David Towner
    Mrs. K.C. Towner
    Miss Edna Tower
    Dr. Frank I. Tower

32. ARRANGEMENT A
    The Jane Miller Shop
    Joseph Millard Corp.
    John Muller & Co.
    Jean Mullins, Inc.

    ARRANGEMENT B
    Joseph Millard Corp.
    The Jane Miller Shop
    John Muller & Co.
    Jean Mullins, Inc.

32.____

    ARRANGEMENT C
    The Jane Miller Shop
    Jean Mullins, Inc.
    John Muller & Co.
    Joseph Millard Corp.

    ARRANGEMENT D
    Joseph Millard Corp.
    John Muller & Co.
    Jean Mullins, Inc.
    The Jane Miller Shop

33.
- ARRANGEMENT A
  Anthony Delaney
  A.M. D'Elia
  A. De Landri
  Alfred De Monte

  ARRANGEMENT B
  Anthony Delaney
  A. De Landri
  A.M. D'Elia
  Alfred De Monte

  ARRANGEMENT C
  A. De Landri
  A.M. D'Elia
  Alfred De Monte
  Anthony Delaney

  ARRANGEMENT D
  A. De Landri
  Anthony Delaney
  A.M. D'Elia
  Alfred De Monte

  33.____

34.
- ARRANGEMENT A
  D. McAllen
  Lewis McBride
  Doris MacAllister
  Lewis T. MacBride

  ARRANGEMENT B
  D. McAllen
  Doris MacAllister
  Lewis McBride
  Lewis T. MacBride

  ARRANGEMENT C
  Doris MacAllister
  Lewis T. MacBride
  D. McAllen
  Lewis McBride

  ARRANGEMENT D
  Doris MacAllister
  D. McAllen
  Lewis T. MacBride
  Lewis McBride

  34.____

35.
- ARRANGEMENT A
  6th Ave. Swim Shop
  The Sky Ski School
  Sport Shoe Store
  23rd Street Salon

  ARRANGEMENT B
  23rd Street Salon
  The Sky Ski School
  6th Ave. Swim Shop
  Sport Shoe Store

  ARRANGEMENT C
  6th Ave. Swim Shop
  Sport Shoe Store
  The Sky Ski School
  23rd Street Salon

  ARRANGEMENT D
  The Sky Ski School
  6th Ave. Swim Shop
  Sport Shoe Store
  23rd Street Salon

  35.____

36.
- ARRANGEMENT A
  Charlotte Stair
  C.B. Stare
  Charles B. Stare
  Elaine La Stella

  ARRANGEMENT B
  C.B. Stare
  Charles B. Stare
  Charlotte Stair
  Elaine La Stella

  ARRANGEMENT C
  Elaine La Stella
  Charlotte Stair
  C.B. Stare
  Charles B. Stare

  ARRANGEMENT D
  Charles B. Stare
  C.B. Stare
  Charlotte Stair
  Elaine La Stella

  36.____

37.
ARRANGEMENT A
John O'Farrell Corp.
Finest Glass Co.
George Fraser Co.
4th Guarantee Bank

ARRANGEMENT B
Finest Glass Co.
4th Guarantee Bank
George Fraser Co.
John O'Farrell Corp.

ARRANGEMENT C
John O'Farrell Corp.
Finest Glass Co.
4th Guarantee Bank
George Fraser Co.

ARRANGEMENT D
Finest Glass Co.
George Fraser Co.
John O'Farrell Corp.
4th Guarantee Bank

37.____

Questions 38-47.

DIRECTIONS: Questions 38 to 47 are based on the Weekly Payroll Record, shown below, of Bureau X in a public agency. In answering these questions, note that gross weekly salary is the salary before deductions have been made; take-home pay is the amount remaining after all indicated weekly deductions have been made from the gross weekly salary. In answering questions involving annual amounts, compute on the basis of 52 weeks per year.

BUREAU X
WEEKLY PAYROLL PERIOD

Unit in Which Employed	Employee	Title	Gross Weekly Salary (Before Deductions)	Medical Insurance	Income Tax	Pension System
Accounting	Allen	Accountant	$950	$14.50	$125.00	$53.20
"	Earth	Bookkeeper	720	19.00	62.00	40.70
"	Keller	Clerk	580	6.50	82.00	33.10
"	Peters	Typist	560	6.50	79.00	35.30
"	Simons	Stenographer	610	14.50	64.00	37.80
Information	Brown	Clerk	560	13.00	56.00	42.22
"	Smith	Clerk	590	14.50	61.00	58.40
"	Turner	Typist	580	13.00	59.00	62.60
"	Williams	Stenographer	620	19.00	44.00	69.40
Mail	Conner	Clerk	660	13.00	74.00	55.40
"	Farrell	Typist	540	6.50	75.00	34.00
"	Johnson	Stenographer	580	19.00	36.00	37.10
Records	Dillon	Clerk	640	6.50	94.00	58.20
"	Martin	Clerk	540	19.00	29.00	50.20
"	Standish	Typist	620	14.50	67.00	60.10
"	Wilson	Stenographer	690	6.50	101.00	75.60

38. Dillon's annual take-home pay is MOST NEARLY

A. $25,000   B. $27,000   C. $31,000   D. $33,000

38.____

39. The difference between Turner's gross annual salary and his annual take-home pay is MOST NEARLY

   A. $3,000   B. $5,000   C. $7,000   D. $9,000

40. Of the following, the employee whose weekly take-home pay is CLOSEST to that of Keller's is

   A. Peters   B. Brown   C. Smith   D. Turner

41. The average gross annual salary of the typists is

   A. less than $27,500
   B. more than $27,500 but less than $30,000
   C. more than $30,000 but less than $32,500
   D. more than $32,500

42. The average gross weekly salary of the stenographers EXCEEDS the gross weekly salary of the clerks by

   A. $20   B. $30   C. $40   D. $50

43. Of the following employees in the Accounting Unit, the one who pays the HIGHEST percentage of his gross weekly salary for the Pension System is

   A. Barth   B. Keller   C. Peters   D. Simons

44. For all of the Accounting Unit employees, the total annual deductions for Medical Insurance are less than the total annual deductions for the Pension System by MOST NEARLY

   A. $6,000   B. $7,000   C. $8,000   D. $9,000

45. Of the following, the employee whose total weekly deductions are MOST NEARLY 27% of his gross weekly salary is

   A. Barth   B. Brown   C. Martin   D. Wilson

46. The total amount of the gross weekly salaries of all the employees in the Records Unit is MOST NEARLY

   A. 95% of the total amount of the gross weekly salaries of all the employees in the Information Unit
   B. 10% greater than the total amount of the gross weekly salaries of all the employees in the Mail Unit
   C. 75% of the total amount of the gross weekly salaries of all the employees in the Accounting Unit
   D. four times as great as the total amount deducted weekly for tax for all the employees in the Records Unit

47. For the employees in the Information Unit, the average weekly deductions for Income Tax   47.____
   A. exceeds the average weekly deduction for Income Tax for the employees in the Records Unit
   B. is less than the average weekly deduction for the Pension System for the employees in the Mail Unit
   C. exceeds the average weekly deduction for Income Tax for the employees in the Accounting Unit
   D. is less than the average weekly deduction for the Pension System for the employees in the Records Unit

Questions 48-50.

DIRECTIONS: Questions 48 to 50 are a test of your proofreading ability. Each question consists of Copy I and Copy II. You are to assume that Copy I in each question is correct. Copy II, which is meant to be a duplicate of Copy I, may contain some typographical errors. In each question, compare Copy II with Copy I and determine the number of errors in Copy II. If there are:
   no errors, mark your answer A;
   1 or 2 errors, mark your answer B;
   3 or 4 errors, mark your answer C;
   5 errors or more, mark your answer D.

48. COPY I   48.____
It shall be unlawful to install wires or appliances for electric light, heat or power, operating at a potential in excess of seven hundred fifty volts, in or on any part of a building, with the exception of a central station, sub-station, transformer, or switching vault, or motor room; provided, however, that the Commissioner may authorize the use of radio transmitting apparatus under special conditions.

COPY II
It shall be unlawful to install wires or appliances for electric light, heat or power, operating at a potential in excess of seven hundred fifty volts, in or on any part of a building, with the exception of a central station, substation, transformer, or switching vault, or motor room, provided, however, that the Commissioner may authorize the use of radio transmitting apparatus under special conditions.

49. COPY I   49.____
The grand total debt service for the fiscal year 2006-07 amounts to $350,563,718.63, as compared with $309,561,347.27 for the current fiscal year, or an increase of $41,002,371.36. The amount payable from other sources in 2006-07 shows an increase of $13,264,165.47, resulting in an increase of $27,733,205.89 payable from tax levy funds.

COPY II
The grand total debt service for the fiscal year 2006-07 amounts to $350,568,718.63, as compared with $309,561,347.27 for the current fiscel year, or an increase of $41,002.371.36. The amount payable from other sources in 2006-07 show an increase of $13,264,165.47 resulting in an increase of $27,733,295.89 payable from tax levy funds.

50. COPY I

The following site proposed for the new building is approximately rectangular in shape and comprises an entire block, having frontages of about 721 feet on 16th Road, 200 feet on 157th Street, 721 feet on 17th Avenue and 200 feet on 154th Street, with a gross area of about 144,350 square feet. The 2006-07 assessed valuation is $28,700 of which $6,000 is for improvements.

COPY II

The following site proposed for the new building is approximetely rectangular in shape and comprises an entire block, having frontage of about 721 feet on 16th Road, 200 feet on 157th Street, 721 feet on 17th Avenue, and 200 feet on 134th Street, with a gross area of about 114,350 square feet. The 2006-07 assessed valuation is $28,700 of which $6,000 is for improvements.

KEY (CORRECT ANSWERS)

1. C	11. A	21. B	31. C	41. B
2. A	12. C	22. C	32. B	42. B
3. B	13. B	23. B	33. D	43. C
4. D	14. D	24. A	34. C	44. B
5. C	15. A	25. A	35. A	45. D
6. A	16. C	26. B	36. C	46. C
7. A	17. A	27. D	37. B	47. D
8. A	18. D	28. D	38. A	48. C
9. D	19. B	29. B	39. C	49. D
10. B	20. C	30. A	40. C	50. D

CLERICAL ABILITIES
EXAMINATION SECTION
TEST 1

DIRECTIONS: Each question or incomplete statement is followed by several suggested answers or completions. Select the one that BEST answers the question or completes the statement. *PRINT THE LETTER OF THE CORRECT ANSWER IN THE SPACE AT THE RIGHT.*

Questions 1-4.

DIRECTIONS: Questions 1 through 4 are to be answered on the basis of the information given below.

The most commonly used filing system and the one that is easiest to learn is alphabetical filing. This involves putting records in an A to Z order, according to the letters of the alphabet. The name of a person is filed by using the following order: first, the surname or last name; second, the first name; third, the middle name or middle initial. For example, *Henry C. Young* is filed under *Y* and thereafter under *Young, Henry C.* The name of a company is filed in the same way. For example, *Long Cabinet Co.* is filed under *L* while *John T. Long Cabinet Co.* is filed under *L* and thereafter under *Long, John T. Cabinet Co.*

1. The one of the following which lists the names of persons in the CORRECT alphabetical order is:
   A. Mary Carrie, Helen Carrol, James Carson, John Carter
   B. James Carson, Mary Carrie, John Carter, Helen Carrol
   C. Helen Carrol, James Carson, John Carter, Mary Carrie
   D. John Carter, Helen Carrol, Mary Carrie, James Carson

1.____

2. The one of the following which lists the names of persons in the CORRECT alphabetical order is:
   A. Jones, John C.; Jones, John A.; Jones, John P.; Jones, John K.
   B. Jones, John P.; Jones, John K.; Jones, John C.; Jones, John A.
   C. Jones, John A.; Jones, John C.; Jones, John K.; Jones, John P.
   D. Jones, John K.; Jones, John C.; Jones, John A.; Jones, John P.

2.____

3. The one of the following which lists the names of the companies in the CORRECT alphabetical order is:
   A. Blane Co., Blake Co., Block Co., Blear Co.
   B. Blake Co., Blane Co., Blear Co., Block Co.
   C. Block Co., Blear Co., Blane Co., Blake Co.
   D. Blear Co., Blake Co., Blane Co., Block Co.

3.____

4. You are to return to the file an index card on *Barry C. Wayne Materials and Supplies Co.*
   Of the following, the CORRECT alphabetical group that you should return the index card to is
   A. A to G   B. H to M   C. N to S   D. T to Z

Questions 5-10.

DIRECTIONS: In each of Questions 5 through 10, the names of four people are given. For each question, choose as your answer the one of the four names given which should be filed FIRST according to the usual system of alphabetical filing of names, as described in the following paragraph.

In filing names, you must start with the last name. Names are filed in order of the first letter of the last name, then the second letter, etc. Therefore, BAILY would be filed before BROWN, which would be filed before COLT. A name with fewer letters of the same type comes first, i.e., Smith before Smithe. If the last names are the same, the names are filed alphabetically by the first name. If the first name is an initial, a name with an initial would come before a first name that starts with the same letter as the initial. Therefore, I. BROWN would come before IRA BROWN. Finally, if both last name and first name are the same, the name would be filed alphabetically by the middle name, once again an initial coming before a middle name which starts with the same letter as the initial. If there is no middle name at all, the name would come before those with middle initials or names.

    SAMPLE QUESTION: A. Lester Daniels
                                              B. William Dancer
                                              C. Nathan Danzig
                                              D. Dan Lester

The last names beginning with D are filed before the last name beginning with L. Since DANIELS, DANCER, and DANZIG all begin with the same three letters, you must look at the fourth letter of the last name to determine which name should be filed first. C comes before I or Z in the alphabet, so DANCER is filed before DANIELS or DANZIG. Therefore, the answer to the above sample question is B.

5.   A. Scott Biala
       B. Mary Byala
       C. Martin Baylor
       D. Francis Bauer

6.   A. Howard J. Black
       B. Howard Black
       C. J. Howard Black
       D. John H. Black

7.   A. Theodora Garth Kingston
       B. Theadore Barth Kingston
       C. Thomas Kingston
       D. Thomas T. Kingston

8. A. Paulette Mary Huerta
    B. Paul M. Huerta
    C. Paulette L. Huerta
    D. Peter A. Huerta

9. A. Martha Hunt Morgan
    B. Martin Hunt Morgan
    C. Mary H. Morgan
    D. Martine H. Morgan

10. A. James T. Meerschaum
    B. James M. Mershum
    C. James F. Mearshaum
    D. James N. Meshum

Questions 11-14.

DIRECTIONS: Questions 11 through 14 are to be answered SOLELY on the basis of the following information.

You are required to file various documents in file drawers which are labeled according to the following pattern:

DOCUMENTS

MEMOS		LETTERS	
File	Subject	File	Subject
84PM1	(A-L)	84PC1	(A-L)
84PM2	(M-Z)	84PC2	(M-Z)

REPORTS		INQUIRIES	
File	Subject	File	Subject
84PR1	(A-L)	84PQ1	(A-L)
84PR2	(M-Z)	84PQ2	(M-Z)

11. A letter dealing with a burglary should be filed in the drawer labeled
    A. 84PM1   B. 84PC1   C. 84PR1   D. 84PQ2

12. A report on Statistics should be found in the drawer labeled
    A. 84PM1   B. 84PC2   C. 84PR2   D. 84PQS

13. An inquiry is received about parade permit procedures. It should be filed in the drawer labeled
    A. 84PM2   B. 84PC1   C. 84PR1   D. 84PQ2

14. A police officer has a question about a robbery report you filed. You should pull this file from the drawer labeled
    A. 84PM1   B. 84PM2   C. 84PR1   D. 84PR2

Questions 15-22.

DIRECTIONS: Each of Questions 15 through 22 consists of four or six numbered names. For each question, choose the option (A, B, C, or D) which indicates the order in which the names should be filed in accordance with the following filing instructions:
- File alphabetically according to last name, then first name, then middle initial.
- File according to each successive letter within a name.
- When comparing two names in which the letters in the longer name are identical to the corresponding letters in the shorter name, the shorter name is filed first.
- When the last names are the same, initials are always filed before names beginning with the same letter.

15. I. Ralph Robinson
    II. Alfred Ross
    III. Luis Robles
    IV. James Roberts

    The CORRECT filing sequence for the above names should be
    A. IV, II, I, III   B. I, IV, III, II   C. III, IV, I, II   D. IV, I, III, II

16. I. Irwin Goodwin
    II. Inez Gonzalez
    III. Irene Goodman
    IV. Ira S. Goodwin
    V. Ruth I. Goldstein
    VI. M.B. Goodman

    The CORRECT filing sequence for the above names should be
    A. V, II, I, IV, III, VI   B. V, II, VI, III, IV, I
    C. V, II, III, VI, IV, I   D. V, II, III, VI, I, IV

17. I. George Allan
    II. Gregory Allen
    III. Gary Allen
    IV. George Allen

    The CORRECT filing sequence for the above names should be
    A. IV, III, I, II   B. I, IV, II, III   C. III, IV, I, II   D. I, III, IV, II

18. I.   Simon Kauffman
     II. Leo Kaufman
     III. Robert Kaufmann
     IV. Paul Kauffmann

     The CORRECT filing sequence for the above names should be
     A. I, IV, II, III   B. II, IV, III, I   C. III, II, IV, I   D. I, II, III, IV

19. I.   Roberta Williams
     II. Robin Wilson
     III. Roberta Wilson
     IV. Robin Williams

     The CORRECT filing sequence for the above names should be
     A. III, II, IV, I   B. I, IV, III, II   C. I, II, III, IV   D. III, I, II, IV

20. I.   Lawrence Shultz
     II. Albert Schultz
     III. Theodore Schwartz
     IV. Thomas Schwarz
     V.   Alvin Schultz
     VI. Leonard Shultz

     The CORRECT filing sequence for the above names should be
     A. II, V, III, IV, I, VI   B. IV, III, V, I, II, VI
     C. II, V, I, VI, III, IV   D. I, VI, II, V, III, IV

21. I.   McArdle
     II. Mayer
     III. Maletz
     IV. McNiff
     V.   Meyer
     VI. MacMahon

     The CORRECT filing sequence for the above names should be
     A. I, IV, VI, III, II, V   B. II, I, IV, VI, III, V
     C. VI, III, II, I, IV, V   D. VI, III, II, V, I, IV

22. I.   Jack E. Johnson
     II. R.H. Jackson
     III. Bertha Jackson
     IV. J.T. Johnson
     V.   Ann Johns
     VI. John Jacobs

     The CORRECT filing sequence for the above names should be
     A. II, III, VI, V, IV, I   B. III, II, VI, V, IV, I
     C. VI, II, III, I, V, IV   D. III, II, VI, IV, V, I

Questions 23-30.

DIRECTIONS: The code table below shows 10 letters with matching numbers. For each question, there are three sets of letters. Each set of letters is followed by a set of numbers which may or may not match their correct letter according to the code table. For each question, check all three sets of letters and numbers and mark your answer:
    A. if no pairs are correctly matched
    B. if only one pair is correctly matched
    C. if only two pairs are correctly matched
    D. if all three pairs are correctly matched

CODE TABLE

T	M	V	D	S	P	R	G	B	H
1	2	3	4	5	6	7	8	9	0

SAMPLE QUESTION: TMVDSP – 123456
                              RGBHTM – 789011
                              DSPRGB – 256789

In the sample question above, the first set of numbers correctly match its set of letters. But the second and third pairs contain mistakes. In the second pair, M is correctly matched with number 1. According to the code table, letter M should be correctly matched with number 2. In the third pair, the letter D is incorrectly matched with number 2. According to the code table, letter D should be correctly matched with number 4. Since only one of the pairs is correctly matched, the answer to this sample question is B.

23.   RSBMRM – 759262   23.____
      GDSRVH – 845730
      VDBRTM - 349713

24.   TGVSDR – 183247   24.____
      SMHRDP – 520647
      TRMHSR - 172057

25.   DSPRGM – 456782   25.____
      MVDBHT – 234902
      HPMDBT - 062491

26.   BVPTRD – 936184   26.____
      GDPHMB – 807029
      GMRHMV - 827032

27.   MGVRSH – 283750   27.____
      TRDMBS – 174295
      SPRMGV - 567283

28. SGBSDM – 489542   28.____
    MGHPTM – 290612
    MPBMHT - 269301

29. TDPBHM – 146902   29.____
    VPBMRS – 369275
    GDMBHM - 842902

30. MVPTBV – 236194   30.____
    PDRTMB – 47128
    BGTMSM - 981232

KEY (CORRECT ANSWERS)

1.	A	11.	B	21.	C
2.	C	12.	C	22.	B
3.	B	13.	D	23.	B
4.	D	14.	D	24.	B
5.	D	15.	D	25.	C
6.	B	16.	C	26.	A
7.	B	17.	D	27.	D
8.	B	18.	A	28.	A
9.	A	19.	B	29.	D
10.	C	20.	A	30.	A

TEST 2

DIRECTIONS: Each question or incomplete statement is followed by several suggested answers or completions. Select the one that BEST answers the question or completes the statement. *PRINT THE LETTER OF THE CORRECT ANSWER IN THE SPACE AT THE RIGHT.*

Questions 1-10.

DIRECTIONS: Questions 1 through 10 each consists of two columns, each containing four lines of names, numbers and/or addresses. For each question, compare the lines in Column I with the lines in Column II to see if they match exactly, and mark your answer A, B, C, or D, according to the following instructions:
    A. all four lines match exactly
    B. only three lines match exactly
    C. only two lines match exactly
    D. only one line matches exactly

<u>COLUMN I</u>   <u>COLUMN II</u>

1.   I.   Earl Hodgson   Earl Hodgson   1.____
     II.   1409870   1408970
     III.   Shore Ave.   Schore Ave.
     IV.   Macon Rd.   Macon Rd.

2.   I.   9671485   9671485   2.____
     II.   470 Astor Court   470 Astor Court
     III.   Halprin, Phillip   Halperin, Phillip
     IV.   Frank D. Poliseo   Frank D. Poliseo

3.   I.   Tandem Associates   Tandom Associates   3.____
     II.   144-17 Northern Blvd.   144-17 Northern Blvd.
     III.   Alberta Forchi   Albert Forchi
     IV.   Kings Park, NY 10751   Kings Point, NY 10751

4.   I.   Bertha C. McCormack   Bertha C. McCormack   4.____
     II.   Clayton, MO   Clayton, MO
     III.   976-4242   976-4242
     IV.   New City, NY 10951   New City, NY 10951

5.   I.   George C. Morill   George C. Morrill   5.____
     II.   Columbia, SC 29201   Columbia, SD 29201
     III.   Louis Ingham   Louis Ingham
     IV.   3406 Forest Ave.   3406 Forest Ave.

6.   I.   506 S. Elliott Pl.   506 S. Elliott Pl.   6.____
     II.   Herbert Hall   Hurbert Hall
     III.   4712 Rockaway Pkway   4712 Rockaway Pkway
     IV.   169 E. 7 St.   169 E. 7 St.

7. I.   345 Park Ave.   345 Park Pl.   7.____
    II.   Colman Oven Corp.   Coleman Oven Corp.
    III. Robert Conte   Robert Conti
    IV.   6179846   6179846

8. I.   Grigori Schierber   Grigori Schierber   8.____
    II.   Des Moines, Iowa   Des Moines, Iowa
    III. Gouverneur Hospital   Gouverneur Hospital
    IV.   91-35 Cresskill Pl.   91-35 Cresskill Pl.

9. I.   Jeffery Janssen   Jeffrey Janssen   9.____
    II.   8041071   8041071
    III. 40 Rockefeller Plaza   40 Rockafeller Plaza
    IV.   407 6 St.   406 7 St.

10. I.   5971996   5871996   10.____
    II.   3113 Knickerbocker Ave.   31123 Knickerbocker Ave.
    III. 8434 Boston Post Rd.   8424 Boston Post Rd.
    IV.   Penn Station   Penn Station

Questions 11-14.

DIRECTIONS: Questions 11 through 14 are to be answered by looking at the four groups of names and addresses listed below (I, II, III, and IV), and then finding out the number of groups that have their corresponding numbered lies exactly the same.

	GROUP I	GROUP II
Line 1.	Richmond General Hospital	Richman General Hospital
Line 2.	Geriatric Clinic	Geriatric Clinic
Line 3.	3975 Paerdegat St.	3975 Peardegat St.
Line 4.	Loudonville, New York 11538	Londonville, New York 11538

	GROUP III	GROUP IV
Line 1.	Richmond General Hospital	Richmend General Hospital
Line 2.	Geriatric Clinic	Geriatric Clinic
Line 3.	3795 Paerdegat St.	3975 Paerdegat St.
Line 4.	Loudonville, New York 11358	Loudonville, New York 11538

1. In how many groups is line one exactly the same?   11.____
        A. Two   B. Three   C. Four   D. None

12. In how many groups is line two exactly the same?   12.____
        A. Two   B. Three   C. Four   D. None

13. In how many groups is line three exactly the same?   13.____
        A. Two   B. Three   C. Four   D. None

3 (#2)

14. In how many groups is line four exactly the same?   14.____
    A. Two   B. Three   C. Four   D. None

Questions 15-18.

DIRECTIONS: Each of Questions 15 through 18 has two lists of names and addresses. Each list contains three sets of names and addresses. Check each of the three sets in the list on the right to see if they are the same as the corresponding set in the list on the left. Mark your answers:
    A. if none of the sets in the right list are the same as those in the left list
    B. if only one of the sets in the right list is the same as those in the left list
    C. if only two of the sets in the right list are the same as those in the left list
    D. if all three sets in the right list are the same as those in the left list

15. Mary T. Berlinger   Mary T. Berlinger   15.____
    2351 Hampton St.   2351 Hampton St.
    Monsey, N.Y. 20117   Monsey, N.Y. 20117

    Eduardo Benes   Eduardo Benes
    483 Kingston Avenue   473 Kingston Avenue
    Central Islip, N.Y. 11734   Central Islip, N.Y. 11734

    Alan Carrington Fuchs   Alan Carrington Fuchs
    17 Gnarled Hollow Road   17 Gnarled Hollow Road
    Los Angeles, CA 91635   Los Angeles, CA 91685

16. David John Jacobson   David John Jacobson   16.____
    178 34 St. Apt. 4C   178 53 St. Apt. 4C
    New York, N.Y. 00927   New York, N.Y. 00927

    Ann-Marie Calonella   Ann-Marie Calonella
    7243 South Ridge Blvd.   7243 South Ridge Blvd.
    Bakersfield, CA 96714   Bakersfield, CA 96714

    Pauline M. Thompson   Pauline M. Thomson
    872 Linden Ave.   872 Linden Ave.
    Houston, Texas 70321   Houston, Texas 70321

17. Chester LeRoy Masterton   Chester LeRoy Masterson   17.____
    152 Lacy Rd.   152 Lacy Rd.
    Kankakee, Ill. 54532   Kankakee, Ill. 54532

    William Maloney   William Maloney
    S. LaCrosse Pla.   S. LaCross Pla.
    Wausau, Wisconsin 52136   Wausau, Wisconsin 52146

    Cynthia V. Barnes   Cynthia V. Barnes
    16 Pines Rd.   16 Pines Rd.
    Greenpoint, Miss. 20376   Greenpoint,, Miss. 20376

4 (#2)

18. Marcel Jean Frontenac Marcel Jean Frontenac 18.____
    8 Burton On The Water 6 Burton On The Water
    Calender, Me. 01471   Calender, Me. 01471

    J. Scott Marsden   J. Scott Marsden
    174 S. Tipton St.   174 Tipton St.
    Cleveland, Ohio   Cleveland, Ohio

    Lawrence T. Haney   Lawrence T. Haney
    171 McDonough St.   171 McDonough St.
    Decatur, Ga. 31304   Decatur, Ga. 31304

Questions 19-26.

DIRECTIONS: Each of Questions 19 through 26 has two lists of numbers. Each list contains three sets of numbers. Check each of the three sets in the list on the right to see if they are the same as the corresponding set in the list on the left. Mark your answers:

    A. if none of the sets in the right list are the same as those in the left list
    B. if only one of the sets in the right list is the same as those in the left list
    C. if only two of the sets in the right list are the same as those in the left list
    D. if all three sets in the right list are the same as those in the left lists

19. 7354183476   7354983476   19.____
    4474747744   4474747774
    5791430231   57914302311

20. 7143592185   7143892185   20.____
    8344517699   8344518699
    9178531263   9178531263

21. 2572114731   257214731   21.____
    8806835476   8806835476
    8255831246   8255831246

22. 331476853821   331476858621   22.____
    6976658532996   6976655832996
    3766042113715   3766042113745

23. 8806663315   88066633115   23.____
    74477138449   74477138449
    211756663666   211756663666

24. 990006966996   99000696996   24.____
     53022219743   53022219843
     4171171117717   4171171177717

25. 24400222433004   24400222433004   25.____
     5300030055000355   5300030055500355
     20000075532002022   20000075532002022

26. 61116664066001116   61116664066001116   26.____
     7111300117001100733   7111300117001100733
     26666446664476518   26666446664476518

Questions 27-30.

DIRECTIONS: Questions 27 through 30 are to be answered by picking the answer which is in the correct numerical order, from the lowest number to the highest number, in each question.

27. A. 44533, 44518, 44516, 44547   27.____
     B. 44516, 44518, 44533, 44547
     C. 44547, 44533, 44518, 44516
     D. 44518, 44516, 44547, 44533

28. A. 95587, 95593, 95601, 95620   28.____
     B. 95601, 95620, 95587, 95593
     C. 95593, 95587, 95601. 95620
     D. 95620, 95601, 95593, 95587

29. A. 232212, 232208, 232232, 232223   29.____
     B. 232208, 232223, 232212, 232232
     C. 232208, 232212, 232223, 232232
     D. 232223, 232232, 232208, 232208

30. A. 113419, 113521, 113462, 113462   30.____
     B. 113588, 113462, 113521, 113419
     C. 113521, 113588, 113419, 113462
     D. 113419, 113462, 113521, 113588

KEY (CORRECT ANSWERS)

1.	C	11.	A	21.	C
2.	B	12.	C	22.	A
3.	D	13.	A	23.	D
4.	A	14.	A	24.	A
5.	C	15.	C	25.	C
6.	B	16.	B	26.	C
7.	D	17.	B	27.	B
8.	A	18.	B	28.	A
9.	D	19.	B	29.	C
10.	C	20.	B	30.	D

NAME AND NUMBER COMPARISONS

COMMENTARY

This test seeks to measure your ability and disposition to do a job carefully and accurately, your attention to exactness and preciseness of detail, your alertness and versatility in discerning similarities and differences between things, and your power in systematically handling written language symbols.

It is actually a test of your ability to do academic and/or clerical work, using the basic elements of verbal (qualitative) and mathematical (quantitative) learning—words <u>and</u> numbers.

EXAMINATION SECTION

TEST 1

DIRECTIONS: Questions 1 through 6 consist of sets of names and addresses. In each question, the name and address in Column II should be an exact copy of the name and address in Column II. *PRINT IN THE SPACE AT THE RIGHT THE LETTER*
      A. if there is a mistake only in the name
      B. if there is a mistake only in the address
      C. if there is a mistake in both name and address
      D. If there is no mistake in either name or address

SAMPLE:
Michael Filbert
456 Reade Street
New York, N.Y. 10013

Michael Filbert
644 Reade Street
New York, N.Y. 10013

Since there is a mistake only in the address, the answer is B.

1. Esta Wong
141 West 68 St.
New York, N.Y. 10023

   Esta Wang
141 West 68 St.
New York, N.Y. 10023
   1.____

2. Dr. Alberto Grosso
3475 12th Avenue
Brooklyn, N.Y. 11218

   Dr. Alberto Grosso
3475 12th Avenue
Brooklyn, N.Y. 11218
   2.____

3. Mrs. Ruth Bortlas
482 Theresa Ct.
Far Rockaway, N.Y. 11691

   Ms. Ruth Bortias
482 Theresa Ct.
Far Rockaway, N.Y. 11169
   3.____

4. Mr. and Mrs. Howard Fox
2301 Sedgwick Ave.
Bronx, N.Y. 10468

   Mr. and Mrs. Howard Fox
231 Sedgwick Ave.
Bronx, N.Y. 10468
   4.____

5. Miss Marjorie Black
223 East 23 Street
New York, N.Y. 10010

   Miss Margorie Black
223 East 23 Street
New York, N.Y. 10010
   5.____

2 (#1)

6. Michelle Herman   Michelle Hermann   6.____
    806 Valley Rd.   806 Valley Dr.
    Old Tappan, N.J. 07675   Old Tappan, N.J. 07675

KEY (CORRECT ANSWERS)

1. A
2. D
3. C
4. B
5. A
6. C

TEST 2

DIRECTIONS: Questions 1 through 6 consist of sets of names and addresses. In each question, the name and address in Column II should be an exact copy of the name and address in Column II. *PRINT IN THE SPACE AT THE RIGHT THE LETTER*
    A. if there is a mistake only in the name
    B. if there is a mistake only in the address
    C. if there is a mistake in both name and address
    D. If there is no mistake in either name or address

1.   Ms. Joan Kelly   Ms. Joan Kielly   1.____
    313 Franklin Ave.   318 Franklin Ave.
    Brooklyn, N.Y. 11202   Brooklyn, N.Y. 11202

2.   Mrs. Eileen Engel   Mrs. Ellen Engel   2.____
    47-24 86 Road   47-24 86 Road
    Queens, N.Y. 11122   Queens, N.Y. 11122

3.   Marcia Michaels   Marcia Michaels   3.____
    213 E. 81 St.   213 E. 81 St.
    New York, N.Y. 10012   New York, N.Y. 10012

4.   Rev. Edward J. Smyth   Rev. Edward J. Smyth   4.____
    1401 Brandeis Street   1401 Brandies Street
    San Francisco, Calif. 96201   San Francisco, Calif. 96201

5.   Alicia Rodriguez   Alicia Rodriquez   5.____
    24-68 81 St.   2468 81 St.
    Elmhurst, N.Y. 11122   Elmhurst, N.Y. 11122

6.   Ernest Eissemann   Ernest Eisermann   6.____
    21 Columbia St.   21 Columbia St.
    New York, N.Y. 10007   New York, N.Y. 10007

KEY (CORRECT ANSWERS)

1. C
2. A
3. D
4. B
5. C
6. A

TEST 3

DIRECTIONS: Questions 1 through 8 consist of names, locations, and telephone numbers. In each question, the name, location and number in Column II should be an exact copy of the name, location, and number in Column I. *PRINT IN THE SPACE AT THE RIGHT THE LETTER*
- A. if there is a mistake in one line only
- B. if there is a mistake in two lines only
- C. if there is a mistake in three lines only
- D. if there are no mistakes in any of the lines

1. Ruth Lang
   EAM Bldg., Room C101
   625-2000, ext. 765

   Ruth Lang
   EAM Bldg., Room C110
   625-2000, ext. 765

   1.____

2. Anne Marie Ionozzi
   Investigations, Room 827
   576-4000, ext. 832

   Anna Marie Ionozzi
   Investigation, Room 827
   566-4000, ext. 832

   2.____

3. Willard Jameson
   Fm C Bldg. Room 687
   454-3010

   Willard Jamieson
   Fm C Bldg. Room 687
   454-3010

   3.____

4. Joanne Zimmermann
   Bldg. SW, Room 314
   532-4601

   Joanne Zimmermann
   Bldg. SW, Room 314
   532-4601

   4.____

5. Carlyle Whetstone
   Payroll Division-A, Room 212A
   262-5000, ext. 471

   Caryle Whetstone
   Payroll Division-A, Room 212A
   262-5000, ext. 417

   5.____

6. Kenneth Chiang
   Legal Council, Room 9745
   (201) 416-9100, ext. 17

   Kenneth Chiang
   Legal Counsel, Room 9745
   (201) 416-9100, ext. 17

   6.____

7. Ethel Koenig
   Personnel Services Div, Rm 433
   635-7572

   Ethel Hoenig
   Personal Services Div, Rm 433
   635-7527

   7.____

8. Joyce Ehrhardt
   Office of Administrator, Rm W56
   387-8706

   Joyce Ehrhart
   Office of Administrator, Rm W56
   387-7806

   8.____

KEY (CORRECT ANSWERS)

1. A
2. C
3. A
4. D
5. B
6. A
7. C
8. B

TEST 4

DIRECTIONS: Each of Questions 1 through 10 gives the identification number and name of a person who has received treatment at a certain hospital. You are to choose the option (A, B, C, or D) which has EXACTLY the same number and name as those given in the question.

SAMPLE QUESTION:
123765 Frank Y. Jones
- A. 123675 Frank Y. Jones
- B. 123765 Frank T. Jones
- C. 123765 Frank Y. Jones
- D. 123765 Frank Y. Jones

The correct answer is D, because it is the only option showing the identification number and name exactly as they are in the sample question.

1. 754898 Diane Malloy
   - A. 745898 Diane Malloy
   - B. 754898 Dion Malloy
   - C. 754898 Diane Malloy
   - D. 754898 Diane Maloy

2. 661818 Ferdinand Figueroa
   - A. 661818 Ferdinand Figeuroa
   - B. 661618 Ferdinand Figueroa
   - C. 661818 Ferdnand Figueroa
   - D. 661818 Ferdinand Figueroa

3. 100101 Norman D. Braustein
   - A. 100101 Norman D. Braustein
   - B. 101001 Norman D. Braustein
   - C. 100101 Norman P. Braustien
   - D. 100101 Norman D. Bruastein

4. 838696 Robert Kittredge
   - A. 838969 Robert Kittredge
   - B. 838696 Robert Kittredge
   - C. 388696 Robert Kittredge
   - D. 838696 Robert Kittridge

5. 243716 Abraham Soletsky
   - A. 243716 Abrahm Soletsky
   - B. 243716 Abraham Solestky
   - C. 243176 Abraham Soletsky
   - D. 243716 Abraham Soletsky

6. 981121 Phillip M. Maas
   - A. 981121 Phillip M. Mass
   - B. 981211 Phillip M. Maas
   - C. 981121 Phillip M. Maas
   - D. 981121 Phillip N. Maas

7. 786556 George Macalusso
   - A. 785656 George Macalusso
   - B. 786556 George Macalusso
   - C. 786556 George Maculusso
   - D. 786556 George Macluasso

8. 639472 Eugene Weber
   - A. 639472 Eugene Weber
   - B. 639472 Eugene Webre
   - C. 693472 Eugene Weber
   - D. 639742 Eugene Weber

2 (#4)

9. 724936 John J. Lomonaco   9.____
   A. 724936 John J. Lomanoco   B. 724396 John L. Lomonaco
   C. 7224936 John J. Lomonaco   D. 724936 John J. Lamonaco

10. 899868 Michael Schnitzer   10.____
   A. 899868 Micheal Schnitzer   B. 898968 Michael Schnizter
   C. 899688 Michael Schnitzer   D. 899868 Michael Schnitzer

KEY (CORRECT ANSWERS)

1.	C	6.	C
2.	D	7.	B
3.	A	8.	A
4.	B	9.	C
5.	D	10.	D

ADDRESS CHECKING

EXAMINATION SECTION
TEST 1

DIRECTIONS: This test is designed to measure your speed and accuracy. You are urged to work both quickly and accurately and to do correctly as many lists as you can in the time allowed. The test consists of lists of pairs of addresses. Circle the letter *A* on your answer sheet if the two addresses are exactly ALIKE in every way. Circle the letter *D* if they are DIFFERENT.

CIRCLE
CORRECT ANSWER

1.	2134 S 20th St	2134 S 20th St	A	D
2.	4608 N Warnock St	4806 N Warnock St	A	D
3.	1202 W Girard Dr	1202 W Girard Rd	A	D
4.	3120 S Harcourt St	3120 S Harcourt St	A	D
5.	4618 W Addison St	4618 E Addison St	A	D
6.	39-B Parkway Rd	39-D Parkway Rd	A	D
7.	6425 N Delancey	6425 N Delancey	A	D
8.	5407 Columbia Rd	5407 Columbia Rd	A	D
9.	2106 Southern Ave	2106 Southern Ave	A	D
10.	Highfalls NC	Highlands NC	A	D
11.	2873 Pershing Dr	2673 Pershing Dr	A	D
12.	1329 N H Ave NW	1329 N J Ave NW	A	D
13.	13 1316 N Quinn St Arl	1316 N Quinn St Alex	A	D
14.	7507 Wyngate Dr	7505 Wyngate Dr	A	D
15.	15 2918 Colesville Rd	2918 Colesville Rd	A	D
16.	16 2071 Belvedere Dr	2071 Belvedere Dr	A	D
17.	Palmer Wash	Palmer Mich	A	D
18.	2106 16th St SW	2106 16th St SW	A	D
19.	64-23 229th St	64-23 229th St	A	D
20.	8744 E St NE	8744 E St NE	A	D
21.	668-15 Lee Dr	668-151 Lee Dr	A	D
22.	84-84 Bay 16 St	84-84 Baye 16 St	A	D
23.	1117 E Egg Lane	11117 E Egg Lane	A	D
24.	36 W Pingrey Dr Easterville Md	36 W Pingrey Dr Easterville Md	A	D
25.	A-34 N 176 Rd NE Doddsville Mich	A-34 N 176 Rd NE Doddsville Mich	A	D

KEY (CORRECT ANSWERS)

1. A
2. D
3. D
4. A
5. D

6. D
7. A
8. A
9. A
10. D

11. D
12. D
13. D
14. D
15. A

16. A
17. D
18. A
19. A
20. A

21. D
22. D
23. D
24. A
25. A

TEST 2

DIRECTIONS: This test is designed to measure your speed and accuracy. You are urged to work both quickly and accurately and to do correctly as many lists as you can in the time allowed. The test consists of lists of pairs of addresses. Circle the letter *A* on your answer sheet if the two addresses are exactly ALIKE in every way. Circle the letter *D* if they are DIFFERENT.

CIRCLE
CORRECT ANSWER

1.	89 Mohicn Pk Ave	89 Mohcn Pk Ave	A	D
2.	355 Warburton Av	355 Waburton Av	A	D
3.	20 Otis Ave	20 Otis Av	A	D
4.	Tutle Dr Osning	Tuttle Dr Osning	A	D
5.	15 South Pl Chapqa	15 South Pl Chapqua	A	D
6.	83 McLean Ave	83 McLean Av	A	D
7.	168 Ellison Ave Bronxvil	168 Ellson Av Bronxvil	A	D
8.	77 Lvngstn Av	79 Lvngstn Ave	A	D
9.	52 1/2 Wstmnstr Dr	52 1/2 Wstmnstr Av	A	D
10.	10 132A Old Crompnd Rd	132A Old Crompond Rd	A	D
11.	581 Bway Hastgs-on-Hdsn	581 Bway Hstg-on-Hdson	A	D
12.	682 Scrsdl Rd NW	682 Scrsdl Rd NW	A	D
13.	109 S Regent Mt Ksco	109 S Regent Mt.Ksco	A	D
14.	151 N Frnch Ave Elmsfrd	151 N Frnch Ave Elmfrd	A	D
15.	12 Gomer Jefrsn Vly	12 Gomar Jefrsn Vly	A	D
16.	391 Plesnt Nw Roch	391 Plesnt NW Roch	A	D
17.	22 1/2A Keogh La	22 1/2A Keoh La	A	D
18.	159 Meetg Hse Rd Bdfrd	15 Meetg Hse Rd Bdfrd	A	D
19.	2131 Shrad Rd Brirclf Mnr	2131 Shrd Rd Brirclf Mnr	A	D
20.	139 Amackasn Ter SE	139 Amckasn Ter SE	A	D

KEY (CORRECT ANSWERS)

1.	D	11.	D
2.	D	12.	A
3.	D	13.	D
4.	D	14.	D
5.	D	15.	D
6.	D	16.	D
7.	D	17.	D
8.	D	18.	D
9.	D	19.	D
10.	D	20.	D

TEST 3

DIRECTIONS: This test is designed to measure your speed and accuracy. You are urged to work both quickly and accurately and to do correctly as many lists as you can in the time allowed. The test consists of lists of pairs of addresses. Circle the letter *A* on your answer sheet if the two addresses are exactly ALIKE in every way. Circle the letter *D* if they are DIFFERENT.

CIRCLE
CORRECT ANSWER

1.	429 Nthn Hale Dr Hntgtn	429 Nthn Hale Dr Htgtn	A	D
2.	111 Shubrt Dr Haupaug	111 Shubrt Dr Haupaug	A	D
3.	156 Somrs La&Indn Hd Rd	167 Somers La & Indn Hd Rd	A	D
4.	1996 Sunst Av Wsthmptn Bch	199 Sunst Av Wsthmptn Bch	A	D
5.	135 W Shincok Rd Quog	135 W Shinck Rd Quog	A	D
6.	1579 B Strght Pth Wyandnch	1579B Strght Pth Wyandich	A	D
7.	1056 Yoakm Av	1056 Yoakum Av	A	D
8.	59 Wohsepe Dr Brghtwtrs	59 Wohsepe Dr Brghtwtrs	A	D
9.	1131A Wlt Whtmn Rd	1131 Wh Whtmn Rd	A	D
10.	137 Conscnce Cir Setukt	137 Consnce Cir Setukt	A	D
11.	941 Duane Dr Lk Rnknkma	941 Duanne Dr Lk Rnknkma	A	D
12.	1896 Hustn Lndnhrst	1896 Hustn Lndnhrst	A	D
13.	187 E Islip Rd W Islip	187 E Islip Rd Islip	A	D
14.	51 Blugras La	51 Bluegras La	A	D
15.	1B Bodtch Pth Cntr Mrich	1B Bodtch Pth Centr Mrich	A	D
16.	158 Grist Ml La Halsite	158 Grist Ml La Hallsite	A	D
17.	161-35 Shendoa Blvd	161-35 Shenendoa Blvd	A	D
18.	11 Mt Sinai-Coram Rd	11 Mt Sinai-Coram Rd	A	D
19.	31-1B Old Northprt Rd & Kngs Pk Rd	31-1B Old Northprt Rd & Kngs Pk Rd	A	D
20.	867 Medfrd Ave	869 Medfrd Ave	A	D

KEY (CORRECT ANSWERS)

1. D
2. A
3. D
4. D
5. D

6. D
7. D
8. A
9. D
10. D

11. D
12. A
13. D
14. D
15. D

16. D
17. D
18. A
19. A
20. D

TEST 4

DIRECTIONS: This test is designed to measure your speed and accuracy. You are urged to work both quickly and accurately and to do correctly as many lists as you can in the time allowed. The test consists of lists of pairs of addresses. Circle the letter *A* on your answer sheet if the two addresses are exactly ALIKE in every way. Circle the letter *D* if they are DIFFERENT.

			CIRCLE CORRECT ANSWER	
1.	2469 Dogwd Av E Medo	2467 Dogwd Av E Medo	A	D
2.	5613 Lakevw Av Rkvl Cntr	5613 Lakevw Av Rkv Cntr	A	D
3.	481 Shlbrn La Nw Hyd Pk	481 Shlbrn La Nw Hyd Pk	A	D
4.	246 Court Ocnsde	246 Cort Ocnsde	A	D
5.	437 Juneau Blvd Wdbry	437 Junaeu Blvd Wdbry	A	D
6.	376 Wood La Levitwn	376 Wood La Levitwn	A	D
7.	69 Aspn Flrl Pk	59 Aspn Flr Pk	A	D
8.	2835 Vilag La N Wntagh	2835 Village La N Wntagh	A	D
9.	3109 Devnshr Dr E Nrwch	3109 Devnshr Dr E Nrwch	A	D
10.	81-64 Yung Pl Wdmr	81-64 Young Pl Wdmr	A	D
11.	84C Muirfld Rd	84C Muirfld Rd	A	D
12.	23 Bamboola Hksvl	23 Bamboola Hksvl	A	D
13.	139D Pninsla Blvd Vly Strm	139 Pninsla Blvd Vly Strm	A	D
14.	187 Wdland Dr Plandom	187 Wdlan Dr Plandom	A	D
15.	3 Renvil Ct Mil Nk	3 Renvil Ct Ml Nk	A	D
16.	619 Cresnt Dr Old Bthpg	619 Crescnt Dr Old Bthpg	A	D
17.	1518 Unqua Rd Maspeqa	1518 Uniqua Rd Maspeqa	A	D
18.	1017 Renselr Av Atl Bch	1017 Renselr Av Atl Bch	A	D
19.	777 Brook Ct N Nw Hyd Pk	777 Brook Ct Nw Hyd Pk	A	D
20.	2016 Revre Rd Rslyn Hts	2016 Revre Rd Rsyln Hts	A	D

KEY (CORRECT ANSWERS)

1. D
2. D
3. A
4. D
5. D

6. A
7. D
8. D
9. A
10. D

11. A
12. A
13. D
14. D
15. D

16. D
17. D
18. A
19. D
20. D

TEST 5

DIRECTIONS: This test is designed to measure your speed and accuracy. You are urged to work both quickly and accurately and to do correctly as many lists as you can in the time allowed. The test consists of lists of pairs of addresses. Circle the letter *A* on your answer sheet if the two addresses are exactly ALIKE in every way. Circle the letter *D* if they are DIFFERENT.

CIRCLE
CORRECT ANSWER

1.	2512 Pascack Rd Prms	2512 Pasack Rd Prms	A	D
2.	157 Wdlnd Dr Wdclf Lk	157 Wdlnd Dr Wdclf Lk	A	D
3.	2416A Andrsn Blvd Bgfd	2416 Andrsn Av Bgfd	A	D
4.	6215 Athlone Ter Rivr Vl	6215 Athlone Ter Rvr Vl	A	D
5.	666 Plsnt Av Up Sadl Riv	666 Plst Av Up Sadl Riv	A	D
6.	999 Elliott Pl Ruth	999 Eliott Pl Ruth	A	D
7.	357 Blauvlt Dr Hrngtn Pk	357 Blauvlt Dr Hrngtn Pk	A	D
8.	61-34 Upland Rd Ramsy	61-34 Upland Rd Rumsy	A	D
9.	1793 Arcadn Wy Plsd	179 Arcadn Wy Plsd	A	D
10.	3117 Lantna Av Engwd	3117 Lantna Av Englwd	A	D
11.	675 Spindler Ter Sd Bk	675 Spindler Ter Sd Bk	A	D
12.	546 Riverview Pl Mahwah	546 Riverview Pl Mawah	A	D
13.	3061 Hack Crist	3061 Hack Crist	A	D
14.	2099 Lemoin Ave Ft Lee	2099 Lamoin Av Ft Lee	A	D
15.	1133 Mnache Av Mmache	1133 Mnache Av Mnanche	A	D
16.	7100 Qn Ann Rd Tea	7100 Qn Ann Rd Tee	A	D
17.	1255 Euclid Ave Rdgfld Pk	1255 Euclid Av Rdgfld Pk	A	D
18.	8013 Godwin Pl Creskl	8031 Godwin Pl Creskl	A	D
19.	38-03A Alwd Pl Fr Ln	38-03A Alwd Pl Fr Ln	A	D
20.	536 Wilkes La Dmnt	536 Willkes La Dmnt	A	D

KEY (CORRECT ANSWERS)

1.	D	11.	A
2.	A	12.	D
3.	D	13.	A
4.	D	14.	D
5.	D	15.	D
6.	D	16.	D
7.	A	17.	D
8.	D	18.	D
9.	D	19.	A
10.	D	20.	D

TEST 6

DIRECTIONS: This test is designed to measure your speed and accuracy. You are urged to work both quickly and accurately and to do correctly as many lists as you can in the time allowed. The test consists of lists of pairs of addresses. Circle the letter *A* on your answer sheet if the two addresses are exactly ALIKE in every way. Circle the letter *D* if they are DIFFERENT.

			CIRCLE CORRECT ANSWER	
1.	7961 Eastern Ave SE	7961 Eastern Ave SE	A	D
2.	3809 20th Rd N	3309 20th Rd N	A	D
3.	Smicksburg Pa	Smithsburg Pa	A	D
4.	Sherman Ct	Sherman Ct	A	D
5.	Richland Ga	Richland La	A	D
6.	8520 Leesburg Pike SE	8520 Leesburg Pike SE	A	D
7.	Genevia Ar	Geneva Ar	A	D
8.	104 W Jefferson St	104 W Jefferson St	A	D
9.	Meandor WV	Meander WV	A	D
10.	6327 W Mari Ct	6327 W Mari Ct	A	D
11.	3191 Draper Dr SE	3191 Draper Dr SW	A	D
12.	1415 W Green Spring Rd	1415 W Green Spring Rd	A	D
13.	Parr In	Parr In	A	D
14.	East Falmouth Ma 02536	East Falmouth Ms 02536	A	D
15.	3016 N St NW	3015 M St NW	A	D
16.	Yukon Mo	Yukon Mo	A	D
17.	7057 Brookfield Plaza	7057 Brookfield Plaza	A	D
18.	Bethel Oh 45106	Bethel Oh 45106	A	D
19.	Littleton NH	Littleton NC	A	D
20.	8909 Bowie Dr	8909 Bowie Dr	A	D

KEY (CORRECT ANSWERS)

1.	A	11.	D
2.	D	12.	A
3.	D	13.	A
4.	A	14.	D
5.	D	15.	D
6.	A	16.	A
7.	D	17.	A
8.	A	18.	A
9.	D	19.	D
10.	A	20.	A

TEST 7

DIRECTIONS: This test is designed to measure your speed and accuracy. You are urged to work both quickly and accurately and to do correctly as many lists as you can in the time allowed. The test consists of lists of pairs of addresses. Circle the letter A on your answer sheet if the two addresses are exactly ALIKE in every way. Circle the letter D if they are DIFFERENT.

CIRCLE
CORRECT ANSWER

1. Colmar Il   Colmar Il   A   D
2. 784 Matthews Dr NE   784 Matthews Dr NE   A   D
3. 2923 John Marshall Dr   2932 John Marshall Dr   A   D
4. 6023 Woodmont Rd   6023 Woodmount Rd   A   D
5. Nolan Tx   Noland Tx   A   D
6. 342 E Lincolnia Rd   342 E Lincolnia Dr   A   D
7. Jane Ca   Jane Ca   A   D
8. 4921 Seminary Rd   4912 Seminary Rd   A   D
9. Ulmers SC   Ullmers SC   A   D
10. 4804 Montgomery Lane SW   48-64 Montgomery Lane SW   A   D
11. 210 E Fairfax Dr   210 W Pairfax Dr   A   D
12. Hanapepe Hi   Hanapepe Hi   A   D
13. 450 La Calle del Punto   450 La Calle del Punto   A   D
14. Walland Tn 37886   Walland Tn 37836   A   D
15. Villamont Va   Villamont Va   A   D
16. 4102 Georgia Ave NW   4102 Georgia Rd NW   A   D
17. Aroch Or   Aroch Or   A   D
18. 6531 N Walton Ave   6531 N Waldon Ave   A   D
19. Jeff Ky   Jeff Ky   A   D
20. Delphos Ia   Delphis Ia   A   D

KEY (CORRECT ANSWERS)

1. A
2. A
3. D
4. D
5. D

6. D
7. A
8. D
9. D
10. A

11. D
12. A
13. A
14. D
15. A

16. D
17. A
18. D
19. A
20. D

FILING
EXAMINATION SECTION
TEST 1

DIRECTIONS: Each of the following questions contains four names. For each question, choose the name that should be FIRST if the four names are to be arranged in alphabetical order in accordance with the Rules for Alphabetical Filing given before. Read these rules carefully. Then, for each question, indicate in the space at the right the letter before the name that should be FIRST in alphabetical order.

SAMPLE QUESTION
A. Jane Earl   (2)
B. James A. Earle (4)
C. James Earl   (1)
D. J. Earle   (3)

The numbers in parentheses show the proper alphabetical order in which these names should be filed. Since the name that should be filed FIRST is James Earl, the answer to the Sample Question is C.

1. A. Majorca Leather Goods   B. Robert Maiorca and Sons   1.____
    C. Maintenance Management Corp.   D. Majestic Carpet Mills

2. A. Municipal Telephone Service   B. Municipal Reference Library   2.____
    C. Municipal Credit Union   D. Municipal Broadcasting System

3. A. Robert B. Pierce   B. R. Bruce Pierce   3.____
    C. Ronald Pierce   D. Robert Bruce Pierce

4. A. Four Seasons Sports Club   B. 14 Street Shopping Center   4.____
    C. Forty Thieves Restaurant   D. 42nd St. Theaters

5. A. Franco Franceschini   B. Amos Franchini   5.____
    C. Sandra Franceschia   D. Lilie Franchinesca

KEY (CORRECT ANSWERS)

1. C
2. D
3. B
4. D
5. C

TEST 2

DIRECTIONS: Each of the following questions contains four names. For each question, choose the name that should be FIRST if the four names are to be arranged in alphabetical order in accordance with the Rules for Alphabetical Filing given before. Read these rules carefully. Then, for each question, indicate in the space at the right the letter before the name that should be FIRST in alphabetical order.

    SAMPLE QUESTION
    A. Jane Earl   (2)
    B. James A. Earle (4)
    C. James Earl   (1)
    D. J. Earle   (3)

The numbers in parentheses show the proper alphabetical order in which these names should be filed. Since the name that should be filed FIRST is James Earl, the answer to the Sample Question is C.

1. A. Alan Carson, M.D.　　B. The Andrew Carlton Nursing Home　　1.____
   C. Prof., Alfred P. Carlton　　D. Mr. A. Peter Carlton

2. A. Chas. A. Denner　　B. H. Jeffrey Dener　　2.____
   C. Charles Denner　　D. Harold Dener

3. A. James C. Maziola　　B. Joseph A. Mazzola　　3.____
   C. James Maziola　　D. J. Alfred Mazzola

4. A. Bureau of Family Affairs　　B. Office of the Comptroller　　4.____
   C. Department of Gas & Electricity　　D. Board of Estimate

5. A. Robert Alan Pearson　　B. John Charles Pierson　　5.____
   C. Robert Allen Pearson　　D. John Chester Pierson

6. A. The Johnson Manufacturing Co.　　B. C.J. Johnston　　6.____
   C. Bernard Johnsen　　D. Prof. Corey Johnstone

7. A. Ninteenth Century Book Shop　　B. Ninth Federal Bank　　7.____
   C. 19th Hole Coffee Shop　　D. 92nd St. Station

8. A. George S. McNeely　　B. Hugh J. Macintosh　　8.____
   C. Mr. G. Stephen McNeally　　D. Mr. H. James Macintosh

KEY (CORRECT ANSWERS)

1. D
2. B
3. C
4. B
5. A
6. C
7. A
8. D

TEST 3

DIRECTIONS: Each of the following questions contains four names. For each question, choose the name that should be LAST if the four names are to be arranged in alphabetical order in accordance with the Rules for Alphabetical Filing given before. Read these rules carefully. Then, for each question, indicate in the space at the right the letter before the name that should be LAST in alphabetical order.

SAMPLE QUESTION
A. Jane Earl   (2)
B. James A. Earle (4)
C. James Earl   (1)
D. J. Earle   (3)

The numbers in parentheses show the proper alphabetical order in which these names should be filed. Since the name that should be filed LAST is James A. Earle, the answer to the Sample Question is B.

1. A. Steiner, Michael   B. Steinblau, Dr. Walter   1.____
    C. Steinet, Gary   D. Stein, Prof. Edward

2. A. The Paper Goods Warehouse B. T. Pane and Sons Inc.   2.____
    C. Paley, Wallace   D. Painting Supplies Inc.

3. A. D'Angelo, F.   B. De Nove, C.   3.____
    C. Daniels, Frank   D. Dovarre, Carl

4. A. Berene, Arnold   B. Berene, Arnold L.   4.____
    C. Beren, Arnold Lee   D. Berene, A.

5. A. Kallinski, Liza   B. Kalinsky, L.   5.____
    C. Kallinky, E.   D. Kallinsky, Elizabeth

6. A. Morgenom, Salvatore   B. Megan, J.   6.____
    C. J. Morgenthal Consultant Services D. Morgan, Janet

7. A. Ritter, G.   B. Ritter, George   7.____
    B. Riter, George H.   D. Ritter, G.H.

8. A. Wheeler, Adele N.   B. Wieler, Ada   8.____
    C. Weiler, Adelaide   D. Wheiler, Adele

9. A. Macan, Toby   B. Maccini, T.   9.____
    C. MacAvoy, Thomas   D. Mackel, Theodore

10. A. Loomus, Kenneth   B. Lomis Paper Supplies   10.____
    C. Loo, N.   D. Loomis Machine Repair Company

KEY (CORRECT ANSWERS)

1. C
2. A
3. D
4. B
5. D
6. C
7. B
8. B
9. D
10. A

———

TEST 4

DIRECTIONS: In the following questions there are five notations numbered 1 through 5 shown in Column I. Each notation is made up of a supplier's name, a contract number, and a date and is to be filed according to the following rules:

First: File in alphabetical order
Second: When two or more notations have the same supplier, file according to the contract number in numerical order beginning with the lowest number.
Third: When two or more notations have the same supplier and contract number, file according to the date beginning with the earliest date.

In Column II the numbers 1 through 5 are arranged in four ways to show different possible orders in which the merchandise information might be filed. Pick the answer (A, B, C, or D) in Column II in which the notations are arranged according to the above filing rules.

SAMPLE QUESTION

COLUMN I
1. Cluney   (4865)   6/17/72
2. Roster   (2466)   5/10/71
3. Altool   (7114)   10/15/72
4. Cluney   (5276)   12/18/71
5. Cluney   (4865)   4/8/72

COLUMN II
A. 2, 3, 4, 1, 5
B. 2, 5, 1, 3, 4
C. 3, 2, 1, 4, 5
D. 3, 5, 1, 4, 2

The correct way to file the notations is:
3. Altool   (7114)   10/15/72
5. Cluney   (4865)   4/8/72
1. Cluney   (4865)   6/17/72
4. Cluney   (5276)   12/18/71
2. Roster   (2466)   5/10/71

The correct filing order is shown by the numbers in front of each name (3, 5, 1, 4, 2). The answer to the Sample Question is the letter in Column II in front of the numbers 3, 5, 1, 4, 2. This answer is D.

1. COLUMN I
    1. Fenten   (38511)   1/4/73
    2. Meadowlane (5020)   11/1/72
    3. Whitehall   (36142)   6/22/72
    4. Clinton   (4141)   5/26/71
    5. Mester   (8006)   4/20/71

    COLUMN II
    A. 3, 5, 2, 1, 4
    B. 4, 1, 2, 5, 3
    C. 4, 2, 5, 3, 1
    D. 5, 4, 3, 1, 2

2. 1. Harvard   (2286)   2/19/70
    2. Parker   (1781)   4/12/71
    3. Lenson   (9044)   6/6/72
    4. Brothers   (38380)   10/11/72
    5. Parker   (41400)   12/20/70

    A. 2, 4, 3, 1, 5
    B. 2, 1, 3, 4, 5
    C. 4, 1, 3, 2, 5
    D. 5, 2, 3, 1, 4

2 (#4)

		COLUMN I			COLUMN II	
3.	1.	Newtone	(3197)	8/22/70	A. 1, 4, 2, 5, 3	3.____
	2.	Merritt	(4071)	8/8/72	B. 4, 2, 1, 5, 3	
	3.	Writebest	(60666)	4/7/71	C. 4, 5, 2, 1, 3	
	4.	Maltons	(34380)	3/30/72	D. 5, 2, 4, 3, 1	
	5.	Merrit	(4071)	7/16/71		
4.	1.	Weinburt	(45514)	6/4/71	A. 4, 5, 2, 1, 3	4.____
	2.	Owntye	(35860)	10/3/71	B. 4, 2, 5, 3, 1	
	3.	Weinburt	(45514)	2/1/71	C. 4, 2, 5, 1, 3	
	4.	Fasttex	(7677)	11/10/71	D. 4, 5, 2, 3, 1	
	5.	Owntye	(4574)	7/17/71		
5.	1.	Premier	(1003)	7/29/70	A. 2, 1, 4, 3, 5	5.____
	2.	Phylson	(0031)	5/5/71	B. 3, 5, 4, 1, 2	
	3.	Lathen	(3328)	10/3/71	C. 4, 1, 2, 3, 5	
	4.	Harper	(8046)	8/18/72	D. 4, 3, 5, 2, 1	
	5.	Lathen	(3328)	12/1/72		
6.	1.	Repper	(46071)	10/14/72	A. 3, 2, 4, 5, 1	6.____
	2.	Destex	(77271)	8/27/72	B. 3, 4, 2, 5, 1	
	3.	Clawson	(30736)	7/28/71	C. 3, 4, 5, 2, 1	
	4.	Destex	(77271)	8/17/71	D. 3, 5, 4, 2, 1	
	5.	Destex	(77271)	4/14/71		

KEY (CORRECT ANSWERS)

1. B
2. C
3. C
4. A
5. D
6. C

TEST 5

DIRECTIONS: Each of the following questions represents five cards to be filed, numbered 1 through 5 shown in Column I. Each card is made up of the employee's name, a work assignment code number shown in parentheses, and the date of this assignment. The cards are to be filed according to the following rules:

First: File in alphabetical order
Second: When two or more cards have the same employee's name, file according to the work assignment number beginning with the lowest number.
Third: When two or more cards have the same employee's name and same assignment number, file according to the assignment date beginning with the earliest date.

Column II shows the cards arranged in four different orders. Pick the answer (A, B, C, or D) in Column II which shows the cards arranged according to the above filing rules.

SAMPLE QUESTION: See Sample Question (with answer) for Test 4.

Now answer the following questions according to these rules.

	COLUMN I			COLUMN II	
1.	1. Prichard (013469) 4/6/21 2. Parks (678941) 2/7/21 3. Williams (551467) 3/6/20 4. Wilson (551466) 8/9/17 5. Stanhope (300014) 8/9/17			A. 5, 4, 3, 2, 1 B. 1, 2, 5, 3, 4 C. 2, 1, 5, 3, 4 D. 1, 5, 4, 3, 2	1._____
2.	1. Ridgeway (623809) 8/11/21 2. Travers (305439) 4/5/17 3. Tayler (818134) 7/5/18 4. Travers (305349) 5/6/20 5. Ridgeway (623089) 10/9/21			A. 5, 1, 3, 4, 2 B. 5, 1, 3, 2, 4 C. 1, 5, 3, 2, 4 D. 1, 5, 4, 2, 3	2._____
3.	1. Jaffe (384737) 2/19/21 2. Inez (859176) 8/8/22 3. Ingrahm (946460) 8/6/19 4. Karp (256146) 5/5/20 5. Ingrahm (946460) 6/4/20			A. 3, 5, 2, 4, 1 B. 3, 5, 2, 1, 4 C. 2, 3, 5, 1, 4 D. 2, 3, 5. 4, 1	3._____
4.	1. Marrano (369421) 7/24/19 2. Marks (652910) 2/23/21 3. Netto (556772) 3/10/21 4. Marks (652901) 2/17/22 5. Netto (556772) 6/17/20			A. 1, 5, 3, 4, 2 B. 3, 5, 4, 2, 1 C. 2, 4, 1, 5, 3 D. 4, 2, 1, 5, 3	4._____

2 (#5)

	COLUMN I			COLUMN II	
5.	1. Abernathy	(712467)	6/23/20	A. 5, 3, 1, 2, 4	5.___
	2. Acevedo	(680262)	6/23/18	B. 5, 4, 2, 3, 1	
	3. Aaron	(967647)	1/17/19	C. 1, 3, 5, 2, 4	
	4. Acevedo	(680622)	5/14/17	D. 2, 4, 1, 5, 3	
	5. Aaron	(967647)	4/1/15		
6.	1. Simon	(645219)	8/19/20	A. 4, 1, 2, 5, 3	6.___
	2. Simon	(645219)	9/2/18	B. 4, 5, 2, 1, 3	
	3. Simons	(645218)	7/7/20	C. 3, 5, 2, 1, 4	
	4. Simms	(646439)	10/12/21	D. 5, 1, 2, 3, 4	
	5. Simon	(645219)	10/16/17		
7.	1. Rappaport	(312230)	6/11/21	A. 4, 3, 1, 2, 5	7.___
	2. Rascio	(777510)	2/9/20	B. 4, 3, 1, 5, 2	
	3. Rappaport	(312230)	7/3/17	C. 3, 4, 1, 5, 2	
	4. Rapaport	(312330)	9/6/20	D. 5, 2, 4, 3, 1	
	5. Rascio	(777501)	7/7/20		
8.	1. Johnson	(843250)	6/8/17	A. 1, 3, 2, 4, 5	8.___
	2. Johnson	(843205)	4/3/20	B. 1, 3, 2, 5, 4	
	3. Johnson	(843205)	8/6/17	C. 3, 2, 1, 4, 5	
	4. Johnson	(843602)	3/8/21	D. 3, 2, 1, 5, 4	
	5. Johnson	(843602)	8/3/20		

KEY (CORRECT ANSWERS)

1.	C	5	A
2.	A	6.	B
3.	C	7.	B
4.	D	8.	D

TEST 6

DIRECTIONS: In each of the following questions there are four groups of names. One of the groups in each question is NOT in correct alphabetic order. Mark the letter of that group next to the number that corresponds to the number of the question.

1. A. Ace Advertising Agency; Acel, Erwin; Ad Graphics; Ade, E.J. & Co.
   B. Advertising Bureau, Inc.; Advertising Guild, Inc.; Advertising Ideas, Inc.; Advertising Sales Co.
   C. Allan Associates; Allen-Wayne, Inc.; Alley & Richards, Inc.; Allum, Ralph
   D. Anderson & Cairnes; Amos Parrish & Co.; Anderson Merrill Co.; Anderson, Milton

   1.____

2. A. Bach, Henry; Badillo, John; Baer, Budd; Bair, Albert
   B. Baker, Lynn; Bakers, Albert; Bailin, Henry; Bakers Franchise Corp.
   C. Bernhardt, Manfred; Bernstein, Jerome; Best, Frank; Benton Associates
   D. Brandford, Edward; Branstatter Associates; Brown, Martel; Browne, Bert

   2.____

3. A. Cone, Robert; Contempo, Bernard; Conti Advertising; Cooper, James
   B. Cramer, Zed; Creative Sales; Crofton, Ada; Cromwell, Samuel
   C. Cheever, Fred; Chernow Advertising; Chenault Associates; Chester, Arthur
   D. Chain Store Advertising; Chair Lawrence & Co.; Chaite, Alexander E.; Chase, Luis

   3.____

4. A. Delahanty, Francis; Dela McCarthy Associates; Delehanty, Kurnit; Delroy, Stewart
   B. Doerfler, B.R.; Doherty, Clifford; Dorchester Apartments; Dorchester, Monroe
   C. Drayer, Stella; Dreher, Norton; Dreyer, Harvey; Dryer, Lester
   D. Duble, Normal; Duevell, William C.; Du Fine, August; Dugan, Harold

   4.____

5. A. Esmond, Walter; Esty, Willia; Ettinger, Carl; Everett, Austin
   B. Enlos, Cartez; Entertainment, Inc.; Englemore, Irwin; Equity Associates
   C. Einhorn, Anna Mrs.; Einhorn, Arlene; Eisele, Mary; Eisele, Minnie Mrs.
   D. Eagen, Roy; Egale, George; Egan, Barrett; Eisen, Henry

   5.____

6. A. Funt, Rand Inc.; Furman, Fainer & Co.; Furman Roth & Co.; Fusco, Frank A.
   B. Friedan, Phillip; Friedman, Mitchell; Friend, Harvey; Friend, Herbert
   C. Folkart Greeting Cards; Food Service; Foote, Cornelius; Foreign Advertising
   D. Finkels, Eliot; Finnerman, John; Finneran, Joseph; Firestone, Albert

   6.____

7. A. Gubitz, Jay; Guild, Dorothy; Gumbiner, B.; Gussow, Leonard
   B. Gore, Smith; Gotham Art, Inc.; Gotham Editors Service; Gotham-Vladimir, Inc.
   C. Georgian, Wolf; Gerdts, H.J.; German News Co.; Germaine, Werner
   D. Gardner, Fred; Gardner, Roy; Garner, Roy; Gaynor & Ducal Inc.

   7.____

2 (#6)

8. A. Howard, E. T.; Howard, Francis; Howson, Allen; Hoyt, Charles   8.____
   B. Houston, Byron; House of Graphics; Rowland, Lynne; Hoyle, Mortimer
   C. Hi-Lite Art Service; Hickerson, J.M.; Hickey, Murphy; Hicks; Gilbert
   D. Hyman, Bram; Hyman, Charles B.; Hyman, Claire; Hyman, Claude

9. A. Idone, Leopold; Ingraham, Evelyn; Ianuzzi, Frank; Itkin, Simon   9.____
   B. Ideas, Inc.; Inter-Racial Press, Inc.; International Association; Iverson, Ford
   C. Il Trionofo; Inwood Bake Shop; Iridor, Rose; Italian Pastry
   D. Ionadi, Anthony Irena, Louise; Iris, Ysabella; Isabelle, Arlia

10. A. Jonas, Myron; Johnstone, John; Jones, Julius; Joptha, Meyer   10.____
    B. Jeanne's Beauty Shoppe; Jeger, Jans; Jem, H.; Jim's Grill
    C. Jacobs, Abraham & Co., Jacobs, Harold A.; Jacobs, Joseph; Jacobs, M.J.
    D. Japan Air Lines; Jensen, Arne; Judson, P.; Juliano, Jeremiah

KEY (CORRECT ANSWERS)

1.	D	6.	D
2.	B	7.	C
3.	C	8.	B
4.	A	9.	A
5.	B	10.	A

TEST 7

DIRECTIONS: Below are ten groups of names, numbered 1 through 10. For each group, three different filing arrangements of the names in the group are given. In only ONE of these arrangements are the names in correct filing order according to standard rules for filing. For each group, select the ONE arrangement, lettered A, B, C, that is CORRECT.

1. Arrangement A
   Nichols, C. Arnold
   Nichols, Bruce
   Nicholson, Arthur

   Arrangement B
   Nichols, Bruce
   Nichols, C. Arnold
   Nicholson, Arthur

   Arrangement C
   Nicholson, Arthur
   Nichols, Bruce
   Nichols, C. Arnold

   1._____

2. Arrangement A
   Schaefer's Drug Store
   Schaefer, Harry T.
   Schaefer Bros.

   Arrangement B
   Schaefer Bros.
   Schaefer, Harry T.
   Schaefer's Drug Store

   Arrangement C
   Schaefer Bros.
   Schaefer's Drug Store
   Schaefer, Harry T.

   2._____

3. Arrangement A
   Adams' Dime Store
   Adami, David
   Adams, Donald

   Arrangement B
   Adami, David
   Adams' Dime Store
   Adams, Donald

   Arrangement C
   Adami, David
   Adams. Donald
   Adams' Dime Store

   3._____

4. Arrangement A
   Newton, Jas. F.
   Newton, Janet
   Newton-Jarvis Law Firm

   Arrangement B
   Newton-Jarvis Law Firm
   Newton, Jas. F.
   Newton, Janet

   Arrangement C
   Newton, Janet
   Newton-Jarvis Law Firm
   Newton, Jas. F.

   4._____

5. Arrangement A
   Radford and Bigelow
   Radford Transfer Co.
   Radford-Smith, Albert

   Arrangement B
   Radford and Bigelow
   Radford-Smith, Albert
   Radford Transfer Co.

   Arrangement C
   Radford Transfer Co.
   Radford and Bigelow
   Radford-Smith, Albert

   5._____

6. Arrangement A
   Trent, Inc.
   Trent Farm Products
   20th Century Film Corp.

   Arrangement B
   20th Century Film Corp.
   Trent Farm Products
   Trent, Inc.

   Arrangement C
   Trent Farm Products
   Trent, Inc.
   20th Century Film Corp.

   6._____

7. Arrangement A
   Morrell, Ralph
   M.R.B. Paper Co.
   Mt. Ranier Hospital

   Arrangement B
   Morrell, Ralph
   Mt. Ranier Hospital
   M.R.B. Paper Co.

   Arrangement C
   M.R.B. Paper Co.
   Morrell, Ralph
   Mt. Ranier Hospital

   7._____

8. Arrangement A
   Vanity Faire Shop
   Van Loon, Charles
   The Williams Magazine Corp.

   Arrangement B
   The Williams Magazine Corp.
   Van Loon, Charles
   Vanity Faire Shop

   Arrangement C
   Van Loon, Charles
   Vanity Faire Shop

   8._____

2 (#7)

9.   Arrangement A   Arrangement B   Arrangement C   9.____
      Crane and Jones Ins. Co.   L.J. Coughtry Mfg. Co.   Little Folks Shop
      Little Folks Shop   Crane and Jones Ins. Co.   L.J. Coughtry Mfg. Co.
      L.J. Coughtry Mfg. Co.   Little Folks Shop   Crane and Jones Ins. Co.

10.   Arrangement A   Arrangement B   Arrangement C   10.____
      South Arlington Garage   N.Y. State Dept. of Audit   State Antique Shop
      N.Y. State Dept. of Audit   and Control   South Arlington Garage
        and Control   South Arlington Garage   N.Y. State Dept. of Audit
      State Antique Shop   State Antique Shop   and Control

KEY (CORRECT ANSWERS)

1.   B   6.   C
2.   C   7.   A
3.   B   8.   A
4.   A   9.   B
5.   B   10.   B

TEST 8

DIRECTIONS: Below are ten groups of names, numbered 1 through 10. For each group, three different filing arrangements of the names in the group are given. In only ONE of these arrangements are the names in correct filing order according to standard rules for filing. For each group, select the ONE arrangement, lettered A, B, C, that is CORRECT.

1. Arrangement A
Gillilan, William
Gililane, Ethel
Gillihane, Harry

    Arrangement B
Gililane, Ethel
Gillihane, Harry
Gillilan, William

    Arrangement C
Gillihane, Harry
Gillilan, William
Gililane, Ethel

    1.____

2. Arrangement A
Stevens, J. Donald
Stevenson, David
Stevens, James

    Arrangement B
Stevenson, David
Stevens, J. Donald
Stevens, James

    Arrangement C
Stevens, J. Donald
Stevens, James
Stevenson, David

    2.____

3. Arrangement A
Brooks, Arthur E.
Brooks, H. Albert
Brooks, H.T.

    Arrangement B
Brooks, H.T.
Brooks, H. Albert
Brooks, Arthur E.

    Arrangement C
Brooks, H. Albert
Brooks, Arthur E.
Brooks, H.T.

    3.____

4. Arrangement A
Lafayette, Earl
Le Grange, Wm. J.
La Roux Haberdashery

    Arrangement B
Le Grange, Wm. J.
La Roux Haberdashery
Lafayette, Earl

    Arrangement C
Lafayette, Earl
La Roux Haberdashery
Le Grange, Wm. J.

    4.____

5. Arrangement A
Mosher Bros.
Mosher's Auto Repair
Mosher, Dorothy

    Arrangement B
Mosher's Auto Repair
Mosher Bros.
Mosher, Dorothy

    Arrangement C
Mosher Bros.
Mosher, Dorothy
Mosher's Auto Repair

    5.____

6. Arrangement A
Ainsworth, Inc.
Ainsworth, George
Air-O-Pad Co.

    Arrangement B
Ainsworth, George
Ainsworth, Inc.
Air-O-Pad Co.

    Arrangement C
Air-O-Pad Co.
Ainsworth, George
Ainsworth, Inc.

    6.____

7. Arrangement A
Peters' Printing Co.
Peerbridge, Alfred
Peters, Paul

    Arrangement B
Peterbridge, Alfred
Peters, Paul
Petters' Printing Co.

    Arrangement C
Peters, Paul
Peters' Printing Co.
Peterbridge, Alfred

    7.____

8. Arrangement A
Sprague-Miller, Elia
Sprague (and) Reed
Sprague Insurance Co.

    Arrangement B
Sprague (and) Reed
Sprague Insurance Co.
Sprague-Miller, Ella

    Arrangement C
Sprague Insurance Co.
Sprague (and) Reed
Sprague-Miller, Ella

    8.____

113

9. Arrangement A
   Ellis, Chalmers Adv.
      Agency
   Ellis, Chas.
   Ellis, Charlotte

   Arrangement B
   Ellis, Chas.
   Ellis, Charlotte
   Ellis, Chalmers Adv.
      Agency

   Arrangement C
   Ellis, Charlotte
   Ellis, Chas.
   Ellis, Chalmers Adv.
      Agency

   9.____

10. Arrangement A
    Adams, Paul
    Five Acres Coffee Shop
    Fielding Adjust. Co.

    Arrangement B
    Five Acres Coffee Shop
    Adams, Paul
    Fielding Adjust. Co.

    Arrangement C
    Adams, Paul
    Fielding Adjust Co.
    Five Acres Coffee Shop

    10.____

KEY (CORRECT ANSWERS)

1.	B	6.	B
2.	C	7.	B
3.	A	8.	C
4.	C	9.	A
5.	B	10.	C

TEST 9

DIRECTIONS: Below in Section A is a diagram representing 40 divisional drawers in alphabetic file, numbered 1 through 40. Below in Section B is a list of 30 names to be filed, numbered 1 through 30, with a drawer number opposite each name, representing the drawer in which it is assumed a file clerk has filed the name.

Determine which are filed CORRECTLY and which are filed INCORRECTLY based on standard rules for indexing and filing. If the name is filed CORRECTLY, print in the space at the right the letter C. If the name is filed INCORRECTLY, print in the space at the right the letter I.

SECTION A

1 Aa-Al	6 Bs-Bz	11 Ea-Er	16 Gp-Gz	21 Kp-Kz	26 Mo-Mz	31 Qa-Qz	36 Ta-Ti
2 Am-Au	7 Ca-Ch	12 Es-Ez	17 Ha-Hz	22 La-Le	27 Na-Nz	32 Ra-Rz	37 Tj-Tz
3 Av-Az	8 Ci-Co	13 Fa-Fr	18 Ia-Iz	23 Lf-Lz	28 Oa-Oz	33 Sa-Si	38 U-V
4 Ba-Bi	9 Cp-Cz	14 Fa-Fz	19 Ja-Jz	24 Ma-Mi	29 Pa-Pr	34 Sj-St	39 Wa-Wz
5 Bj-Br	10 Da-Dz	15 Ga-Go	20 Ka-Ko	25 Mj-Mo	30 Ps-Pz	35 Su-Sz	40 X-Y-Z

SECTION B

	Name or Title	Drawer No.	
1.	William O'Dea	28	1.____
2.	J. Arthur Crawford	8	2.____
3.	DuPont Chemical Co.	10	3.____
4.	Arnold Bros. Mfg. Co.	2	4.____
5.	Dr. Charles Ellis	10	5.____
6.	Gray and Doyle Adv. Agency	16	6.____
7.	Tom's Smoke Shop	37	7.____
8.	Wm. E. Jarrett Motor Corp.	39	8.____
9.	Penn-York Air Service	29	9.____
10.	Corinne La Fleur	13	10.____
11.	Cartright, Incorporated	7	11.____

2 (#9)

12.	7th Ave. Market	24	12.____
13.	Ft. Schuyler Apts.	13	13.____
14.	Madame Louise	23	14.____
15.	Commerce Dept., U.S. Govt.	38	15.____
16.	Norman Bulwer-Lytton	6	16.____
17.	Hilton Memorial Library	17	17.____
18.	The Linen Chest Gift Shop	36	18.____
19.	Ready Mix Supply Co.	32	19.____
20.	City Service Taxi	8	20.____
21.	A.R.C. Transportation Co.	37	21.____
22.	New Jersey Insurance Co.	19	22.____
23.	Capt. Larry Keith	20	23.____
24.	Girl Scouts Council	15	24.____
25.	University of Michigan	24	25.____
26.	Sister Ursula	38	26.____
27.	Am. Legion Post #9	22	27.____
28.	Board of Hudson River Reg. Dist.	17	28.____
29.	Mid West Bus Lines	39	29.____
30.	South West Tours, Inc.	34	30.____

KEY (CORRECT ANSWERS)

1.	C	11.	C	21.	I
2.	I	12.	I	22.	I
3.	C	13.	C	23.	C
4.	C	14.	I	24.	C
5.	I	15.	C	25.	I
6.	C	16.	C	26.	I
7.	C	17.	C	27.	I
8.	I	18.	I	28.	C
9.	C	19.	C	29.	I
10.	I	20.	C	30.	C

TEST 10

DIRECTIONS: Each question or incomplete statement is followed by several suggested answers or completions. Select the one that BEST answers the question or completes the statement. *PRINT THE LETTER OF THE CORRECT ANSWER IN THE SPACE AT THE RIGHT.*

1. Of the following statements about the numeric system of filing, the one which is CORRECT is that it
    A. is the least accurate of all methods of filing
    B. eliminates the need for cross-referencing
    C. allows for very limited expansion
    D. requires a separate index

2. When more than one name or subject is involved in a piece of correspondence to be filed, the office assistant should GENERALLY
    A. prepare a cross-reference sheet
    B. establish a geographical filing system
    C. prepare out-guides
    D. establish a separate index card for noting such correspondence

3. A tickler file is MOST generally used for
    A. identification of material contained in a numeric file
    B. maintenance of a current listing of telephone numbers
    C. follow-up of matters requiring future attention
    D. control of records borrowed or otherwise removed from the file

4. In filing, the name Ms. "Ann Catalana-Moss" should GENERALLY be indexed as
    A. Moss, Catalana, Ann (Ms.)   B. Catalana-Moss, Ann (Ms.)
    C. Ann Catalana-Moss (Ms.)   D. Moss-Catalana, Ann (Ms.)

5. An office assistant has a set of four cards, each of which contains one of the following names.
   In alphabetic filing, the FIRST of the cards to be filed is
    A. (Ms.) Alma John
    B. Mrs. John (Patricia) Edwards
    C. John-Edward School Supplies, Inc.
    D. John H. Edwards

6. Generally, of the following, the name to be filed FIRST in an alphabetical filing system is
    A. Diane Maestro   B. Diana McElroy
    C. James Mackell   D. James McKell

7. According to generally recognized rules of filing in an alphabetic filing system, the one of the following names which normally should be filed LAST is
   A. Department of Education, New York State
   B. F. B. I.
   C. Police Department of New York City
   D. P.S. 81 of New York City

KEY (CORRECT ANSWERS)

1. D
2. A
3. C
4. B
5. D
6. C
7. B

READING COMPREHENSION
UNDERSTANDING AND INTERPRETING WRITTEN MATERIAL
EXAMINATION SECTION
TEST 1

DIRECTIONS: Each question or incomplete statement is followed by several suggested answers or completions. Select the one that BEST answers the question or completes the statement. *PRINT THE LETTER OF THE CORRECT ANSWER IN THE SPACE AT THE RIGHT.*

Questions 1-3.

DIRECTIONS: Questions 1 through 3 are to be answered SOLELY on the basis of the following statement.

    The equipment in a mailroom may include a mail metering machine. This machine simultaneously stamps, postmarks, seals, and counts letters as fast as the operator can feed them. It can also print the proper postage directly on a gummed strip to be affixed to bulky items. It is equipped with a meter which is removed from the machine and sent to the postmaster to be set for a given number of stampings of any denomination. The setting of the meter must be paid for in advance. One of the advantages of metered mail is that it bypasses the cancellation operation and thereby facilitates handling by the post office. Mail metering also makes the pilfering of stamps impossible, but does not prevent the passage of personal mail in company envelopes through the meters unless there is established a rigid control or censorship over outgoing mail.

1. According to this statement, the postmaster

    A. is responsible for training new clerks in the use of mail metering machines
    B. usually recommends that both large and small firms adopt the use of mail metering machines
    C. is responsible for setting the meter to print a fixed number of stampings
    D. examines the mail metering machine to see that they are properly installed in the mailroom

1.____

2. According to this statement, the use of mail metering machines

    A. requires the employment of more clerks in a mailroom than does the use of postage stamps
    B. interferes with the handling of large quantities of outgoing mail
    C. does not prevent employees from sending their personal letters at company expense
    D. usually involves smaller expenditures for mailroom equipment than does the use of postage stamps

2.____

3. On the basis of this statement, it is MOST accurate to state that

    A. mail metering machines are often used for opening envelopes
    B. postage stamps are generally used when bulky packages are to be mailed
    C. the use of metered mail tends to interfere with rapid mail handling by the post office
    D. mail metering machines can seal and count letters at the same time

3.____

Questions 4-5.

DIRECTIONS: Questions 4 and 5 are to be answered SOLELY on the basis of the following statement.

Forms are printed sheets of paper on which information is to be entered. While what is printed on the form is most important, the kind of paper used in making the form is also important. The kind of paper should be selected with regard to the use to which the form will be subjected. Printing a form on an unnecessarily expensive grade of papers is wasteful. On the other hand, using too cheap or flimsy a form can materially interfere with satisfactory performance of the work the form is being planned to do. Thus, a form printed on both sides normally requires a heavier paper than a form printed only on one side. Forms to be used as permanent records, or which are expected to have a very long life in files, requires a quality of paper which will not disintegrate or discolor with age. A form which will go through a great deal of handling requires a strong, tough paper, while thinness is a necessary qualification where the making of several copies of a form will be required.

4. According to this statement, the type of paper used for making forms

    A. should be chosen in accordance with the use to which the form will be put
    B. should be chosen before the type of printing to be used has been decided upon
    C. is as important as the information which is printed on it
    D. should be strong enough to be used for any purpose

5. According to this statement, forms that are

    A. printed on both sides are usually economical and desirable
    B. to be filed permanently should not deteriorate as time goes on
    C. expected to last for a long time should be handled carefully
    D. to be filed should not be printed on inexpensive paper

Questions 6-8.

DIRECTIONS: Questions 6 through 8 are to be answered SOLELY on the basis of the following paragraph.

The increase in the number of public documents in the last two centuries closely matches the increase in population in the United States. The great number of public documents has become a serious threat to their usefulness. It is necessary to have programs which will reduce the number of public documents that are kept and which will, at the same time, assure keeping those that have value. Such programs need a great deal of thought to have any success.

6. According to the above paragraph, public documents may be LESS useful if

    A. the files are open to the public
    B. the record room is too small
    C. the copying machine is operated only during normal working hours
    D. too many records are being kept

7. According to the above paragraph, the growth of the population in the United States has matched the growth in the quantity of public documents for a period of MOST NEARLY _____ years.

    A. 50   B. 100   C. 200   D. 300

8. According to the above paragraph, the increased number of public documents has made it necessary to

    A. find out which public documents are worth keeping
    B. reduce the great number of public documents by decreasing government services
    C. eliminate the copying of all original public documents
    D. avoid all new copying devices

Questions 9-10.

DIRECTIONS: Questions 9 and 10 are to be answered SOLELY on the basis of the following paragraph.

The work goals of an agency can best be reached if the employees understand and agree with these goals. One way to gain such understanding and agreement is for management to encourage and seriously consider suggestions from employees in the setting of agency goals.

9. On the basis of the above paragraph, the BEST way to achieve the work goals of an agency is to

    A. make certain that employees work as hard as possible
    B. study the organizational structure of the agency
    C. encourage employees to think seriously about the agency's problems
    D. stimulate employee understanding of the work goals

10. On the basis of the above paragraph, understanding and agreement with agency goals can be gained by

    A. allowing the employees to set agency goals
    B. reaching agency goals quickly
    C. legislative review of agency operations
    D. employee participation in setting agency goals

Questions 11-13.

DIRECTIONS: Questions 11 through 13 are to be answered SOLELY on the basis of the following paragraph.

In order to organize records properly, it is necessary to start from their very beginning and trace each copy of the record to find out how it is used, how long it is used, and what may finally be done with it. Although several copies of the record are made, one copy should be marked as the copy of record. This is the formal legal copy, held to meet the requirements of the law. The other copies may be retained for brief periods for reference purposes, but these copies should not be kept after their usefulness as reference ends. There is another reason for tracing records through the office and that is to determine how long it takes the copy of record to reach the central file. The copy of record must not be kept longer than necessary by the section of the office which has prepared it, but should be sent to the central file as soon as possible so that it can be available to the various sections of the office. The central file can make the copy of record available to the various sections of the office at an early date only if it arrives at the central file as quickly as possible. Just as soon as its immediate or active service period is ended, the copy of record should be removed from the central file and put into the inactive file in the office to be stored for whatever length of time may be necessary to meet legal requirements, and then destroyed.

11. According to the above paragraph, a reason for tracing records through an office is to

    A. determine how long the central file must keep the records
    B. organize records properly
    C. find out how many copies of each record are required
    D. identify the copy of record

12. According to the above paragraph, in order for the central file to have the copy of record available as soon as possible for the various sections of the office, it is MOST important that the

    A. copy of record to be sent to the central file meets the requirements of the law
    B. copy of record is not kept in the inactive file too long
    C. section preparing the copy of record does not unduly delay in sending it to the central file
    D. central file does not keep the copy of record beyond its active service period

13. According to the above paragraph, the length of time a copy of a record is kept in the inactive file of an office depends CHIEFLY on the

    A. requirements of the law
    B. length of time that is required to trace the copy of record through the office
    C. use that is made of the copy of record
    D. length of the period that the copy of record is used for reference purposes

Questions 14-16.

DIRECTIONS: Questions 14 through 16 are to be answered SOLELY on the basis of the following paragraph.

The office was once considered as nothing more than a focal point of internal and external correspondence. It was capable only of dispatching a few letters upon occasion and of preparing records of little practical value. Under such a concept, the vitality of the office force was impaired. Initiative became stagnant, and the lot of the office worker was not likely to be a happy one. However, under the new concept of office management, the possibilities of waste and mismanagement in office operation are now fully recognized, as are the possibilities for the modern office to assist in the direction and control of business operations. Fortunately, the modern concept of the office as a centralized service-rendering unit is gaining ever greater acceptance in today's complex business world, for without the modern office, the production wheels do not turn and the distribution of goods and services is not possible.

14. According to the above paragraph, the fundamental difference between the old and the new concept of the office is the change in the   14.____

    A. accepted functions of the office
    B. content and the value of the records kept
    C. office methods and systems
    D. vitality and morale of the office force

15. According to the above paragraph, an office operated today under the old concept of the office MOST likely would   15.____

    A. make older workers happy in their jobs
    B. be part of an old thriving business concern
    C. have a passive role in the conduct of a business enterprise
    D. attract workers who do not believe in modern methods

16. Of the following, the MOST important implication of the above paragraph is that a present-day business organization cannot function effectively without the   16.____

    A. use of modern office equipment
    B. participation and cooperation of the office
    C. continued modernization of office procedures
    D. employment of office workers with skill and initiative

Questions 17-20.

DIRECTIONS: Questions 17 through 20 are to be answered SOLELY on the basis of the following paragraph.

A report is frequently ineffective because the person writing it is not fully acquainted with all the necessary details before he actually starts to construct the report. All details pertaining to the subject should be known before the report is started. If the essential facts are not known, they should be investigated. It is wise to have essential facts written down rather than to depend too much on memory, especially if the facts pertain to such matters as amounts, dates, names of persons, or other specific data. When the necessary information has been gathered, the general plan and content of the report should be thought out before the writing is actually begun. A person with little or no experience in writing reports may find that it is wise to make a brief outline. Persons with more experience should not need a written outline, but they should make mental notes of the steps they are to follow. If writing reports without dictation is a regular part of an office worker's duties, he should set aside a certain time during the day when he is least likely to be interrupted. That may be difficult, but in most offices there are certain times in the day when the callers, telephone calls, and other interruptions are not numerous. During those times, it is best to write reports that need undivided concentration. Reports that are written amid a series of interruptions may be poorly done.

17. Before starting to write an effective report, it is necessary to   17.____

    A. memorize all specific information
    B. disregard ambiguous data
    C. know all pertinent information
    D. develop a general plan

18. Reports dealing with complex and difficult material should be

    A. prepared and written by the supervisor of the unit
    B. written when there is the least chance of interruption
    C. prepared and written as part of regular office routine
    D. outlined and then dictated

19. According to the paragraph, employees with no prior familiarity in writing reports may find it helpful to

    A. prepare a brief outline
    B. mentally prepare a synopsis of the report's content
    C. have a fellow employee help in writing the report
    D. consult previous reports

20. In writing a report, needed information which is unclear should be

    A. disregarded
    B. memorized
    C. investigated
    D. gathered

Questions 21-25.

DIRECTIONS: Questions 21 through 25 are to be answered SOLELY on the basis of the following passage.

    Positive discipline minimizes the amount of personal supervision required and aids in the maintenance of standards. When a new employee has been properly introduced and carefully instructed, when he has come to know the supervisor and has confidence in the supervisor's ability to take care of him, when he willingly cooperates with the supervisor, that employee has been under positive discipline and can be put on his own to produce the quantity and quality of work desired. Negative discipline, the fear of transfer to a less desirable location, for example, to a limited extent may restrain certain individuals from overt violation of rules and regulations governing attendance and conduct which in governmental agencies are usually on at least an agency-wide basis. Negative discipline may prompt employees to perform according to certain rules to avoid a penalty such as, for example, docking for tardiness.

21. According to the above passage, it is reasonable to assume that in the area of discipline, the first-line supervisor in a governmental agency has GREATER scope for action in

    A. *positive* discipline, because negative discipline is largely taken care of by agency rules and regulations
    B. *negative* discipline, because rules and procedures are already fixed and the supervisor can rely on them
    C. *positive* discipline, because the supervisor is in a position to recommend transfers
    D. *negative* discipline, because positive discipline is reserved for people on a higher supervisory level

22. In order to maintain positive discipline of employees under his supervision, it is MOST important for a supervisor to

    A. assure each employee that he has nothing to worry about
    B. insist at the outset on complete cooperation from employees

C. be sure that each employee is well trained in his job
D. inform new employees of the penalties for not meeting standards

23. According to the above passage, a feature of negative discipline is that it   23.____

    A. may lower employee morale
    B. may restrain employees from disobeying the rules
    C. censures equal treatment of employees
    D. tends to create standards for quality of work

24. A REASONABLE conclusion based on the above passage is that positive discipline benefits a supervisor because   24.____

    A. he can turn over orientation and supervision of a new employee to one of his subordinates
    B. subordinates learn to cooperate with one another when working on an assignment
    C. it is easier to administer
    D. it cuts down, in the long run, on the amount of time the supervisor needs to spend on direct supervision

25. Based on the above passage, it is REASONABLE to assume, that an important difference between positive discipline and negative discipline is that positive discipline   25.____

    A. is concerned with the quality of work and negative discipline with the quantity of work
    B. leads to a more desirable basis for motivation of the employee
    C. is more likely to be concerned with agency rules and regulations
    D. uses fear while negative discipline uses penalties to prod employees to adequate performance

KEY (CORRECT ANSWERS)

1. C	11. B
2. C	12. C
3. D	13. A
4. A	14. A
5. B	15. C
6. D	16. B
7. C	17. C
8. A	18. B
9. D	19. A
10. D	20. B

21. A
22. C
23. B
24. D
25. B

TEST 2

Questions 1-6.

DIRECTIONS: Questions 1 through 6 are to be answered SOLELY on the basis of the following passage.

Inherent in all organized endeavors is the need to resolve the individual differences involved in conflict. Conflict may be either a positive or negative factor since it may lead to creativity, innovation and progress on the one hand, or it may result, on the other hand, in a deterioration or even destruction of the organization. Thus, some forms of conflict are desirable, whereas others are undesirable and ethically wrong.

There are three management strategies which deal with interpersonal conflict. In the *divide-and-rule strategy,* management attempts to maintain control by limiting the conflict to those directly involved and preventing their disagreement from spreading to the larger group. The *suppression-of-differences strategy* entails ignoring conflicts or pretending they are irrelevant. In the *working-through-differences strategy,* management actively attempts to solve or resolve intergroup or interpersonal conflicts. Of the three strategies, only the last directly attacks and has the potential for eliminating the causes of conflict. An essential part of this strategy, however, is its employment by a committed and relatively mature management team.

1. According to the above passage, the *divide-and-rule strategy tor* dealing with conflict is the attempt to

    A. involve other people in the conflict
    B. restrict the conflict to those participating in it
    C. divide the conflict into positive and negative factors
    D. divide the conflict into a number of smaller ones

2. The word *conflict* is used in relation to both positive and negative factors in this passage. Which one of the following words is MOST likely to describe the activity which the word *conflict,* in the sense of the passage, implies?

    A. Competition   B. Confusion
    C. Cooperation   D. Aggression

3. According to the above passage, which one of the following characteristics is shared by both the *suppression-of-differences strategy* and the *divide-and-rule strategy?*

    A. Pretending that conflicts are irrelevant
    B. Preventing conflicts from spreading to the group situation
    C. Failure to directly attack the causes of conflict
    D. Actively attempting to resolve interpersonal conflict

4. According to the above passage, the successful resolution of interpersonal conflict requires

    A. allowing the group to mediate conflicts between two individuals
    B. division of the conflict into positive and negative factors
    C. involvement of a committed, mature management team
    D. ignoring minor conflicts until they threaten the organization

2 (#2)

5. Which can be MOST reasonably inferred from the above passage? Conflict between two individuals is LEAST likely to continue when management uses

   A. the *working-through differences strategy*
   B. the *suppression-of differences strategy*
   C. the *divide-and-rule strategy*
   D. a combination of all three strategies

5.____

6. According to the above passage, a DESIRABLE result of conflict in an organization is when conflict

   A. exposes production problems in the organization
   B. can be easily ignored by management
   C. results in advancement of more efficient managers
   D. leads to development of new methods

6.____

Questions 7-13.

DIRECTIONS: Questions 7 through 13 are to be answered SOLELY on the basis of the passage below.

Modern management places great emphasis on the concept of communication. The communication process consists of the steps through which an idea or concept passes from its inception by one person, the sender, until it is acted upon by another person, the receiver. Through an understanding of these steps and some of the possible barriers that may occur, more effective communication may be achieved. The first step in the communication process is ideation by the sender. This is the formation of the intended content of the message he wants to transmit. In the next step, encoding, the sender organizes his ideas into a series of symbols designed to communicate his message to his intended receiver. He selects suitable words or phrases that can be understood by the receiver, and he also selects the appropriate media to be used—for example, memorandum, conference, etc. The third step is transmission of the encoded message through selected channels in the organizational structure. In the fourth step, the receiver enters the process by tuning in to receive the message. If the receiver does not function, however, the message is lost. For example, if the message is oral, the receiver must be a good listener. The fifth step is decoding of the message by the receiver, as for example, by changing words into ideas. At this step, the decoded message may not be the same idea that the sender originally encoded because the sender and receiver have different perceptions regarding the meaning of certain words. Finally, the receiver acts or responds. He may file the information, ask for more information, or take other action. There can be no assurance, however, that communication has taken place unless there is some type of feedback to the sender in the form of an acknowledgement that the message was received.

7. According to the above passage, *ideation* is the process by which the

   A. sender develops the intended content of the message
   B. sender organizes his ideas into a series of symbols
   C. receiver tunes in to receive the message
   D. receiver decodes the message

7.____

8. In the last sentence of the passage, the word *feedback* refers to the process by which the sender is assured that the

    A. receiver filed the information
    B. receiver's perception is the same as his own
    C. message was received
    D. message was properly interpreted

9. Which one of the following BEST shows the order of the steps in the communication process as described in the passage?

    A. 1 - ideation   2 - encoding
       3 - decoding   4 - transmission
       5 - receiving   6 - action
       7 - feedback to the sender

    B. 1 - ideation   2 - encoding
       3 - transmission   4 - decoding
       5 - receiving   6 - action
       7 - feedback to the sender

    C. 1 - ideation   2 - decoding
       3 - transmission   4 - receiving
       5 - encoding   6 - action
       7 - feedback to the sender

    D. 1 - ideation   2 - encoding
       3 - transmission   4 - receiving
       5 - decoding   6 - action
       7 - feedback to the sender

10. Which one of the following BEST expresses the main theme of the passage?

    A. Different individuals have the same perceptions regarding the meaning of words.
    B. An understanding of the steps in the communication process may achieve better communication.
    C. Receivers play a passive role in the communication process.
    D. Senders should not communicate with receivers who transmit feedback.

11. The above passage implies that a receiver does NOT function properly when he

    A. transmits feedback   B. files the information
    C. is a poor listener   D. asks for more information

12. Which one of the following, according to the above passage, is included in the SECOND step of the communication process?

    A. Selecting the appropriate media to be used in transmission
    B. Formulation of the intended content of the message
    C. Using appropriate media to respond to the receiver's feedback
    D. Transmitting the message through selected channels in the organization

13. The above passage implies that the *decoding process* is MOST NEARLY the reverse of the _____ process.

    A. transmission   B. receiving
    C. feedback   D. encoding

Questions 14-19.

DIRECTIONS: Questions 14 through 19 are to be answered SOLELY on the basis of the following passage.

It is often said that no system will work if the people who carry it out do not want it to work. In too many cases, a departmental reorganization that seemed technically sound and economically practical has proved to be a failure because the planners neglected to take the human factor into account. The truth is that employees are likely to feel threatened when they learn that a major change is in the wind. It does not matter whether or not the change actually poses a threat to an employee; the fact that he believes it does or fears it might is enough to make him feel insecure. Among the dangers he fears, the foremost is the possibility that his job may cease to exist and that he may be laid off or shunted into a less skilled position at lower pay. Even if he knows that his own job category is secure, however, he is likely to fear losing some of the important intangible advantages of his present position—for instance, he may fear that he will be separated from his present companions and thrust in with a group of strangers, or that he will find himself in a lower position on the organizational ladder if a new position is created above his.

It is important that management recognize these natural fears and take them into account in planning any kind of major change. While there is no cut-and-dried formula for preventing employee resistance, there are several steps that can be taken to reduce employees' fears and gain their cooperation. First, unwarranted fears can be dispelled if employees are kept informed of the planning from the start and if they know exactly what to expect. Next, assurance on matters such as retraining, transfers, and placement help should be given as soon as it is clear what direction the reorganization will take. Finally, employees' participation in the planning should be actively sought. There is a great psychological difference between feeling that a change is being forced upon one from the outside, and feeling that one is an insider who is helping to bring about a change.

14. According to the above passage, employees who are not in real danger of losing their jobs because of a proposed reorganization

    A. will be eager to assist in the reorganization
    B. will pay little attention to the reorganization
    C. should not be taken into account in planning the reorganization
    D. are nonetheless likely to feel threatened by the reorganization

14.____

15. The passage mentions the *intangible advantages* of a position.
Which of the following BEST describes the kind of advantages alluded to in the passage?

    A. Benefits such as paid holidays and vacations
    B. Satisfaction of human needs for things like friendship and status
    C. Qualities such as leadership and responsibility
    D. A work environment that meets satisfactory standards of health and safety

15.____

16. According to the passage, an employee's fear that a reorganization may separate him from his present companions is a (n)

    A. childish and immature reaction to change
    B. unrealistic feeling since this is not going to happen

16.____

C. possible reaction that the planners should be aware of
D. incentive to employees to participate in the planning

17. On the basis of the above passage, it would be DESIRABLE, when planning a departmental reorganization, to

    A. be governed by employee feelings and attitudes
    B. give some employees lower positions
    C. keep employees informed
    D. lay off those who are less skilled

18. What does the passage say can be done to help gain employees' cooperation in a reorganization?

    A. Making sure that the change is technically sound, that it is economically practical, and that the human factor is taken into account
    B. Keeping employees fully informed, offering help in fitting them into new positions, and seeking their participation in the planning
    C. Assuring employees that they will not be laid off, that they will not be reassigned to a group of strangers, and that no new positions will be created on the organization ladder
    D. Reducing employees' fears, arranging a retraining program, and providing for transfers

19. Which of the following suggested titles would be MOST appropriate for this passage?

    A. PLANNING A DEPARTMENTAL REORGANIZATION
    B. WHY EMPLOYEES ARE AFRAID
    C. LOOKING AHEAD TO THE FUTURE
    D. PLANNING FOR CHANGE: THE HUMAN FACTOR

Questions 20-22.

DIRECTIONS: Questions 20 through 22 are to be answered SOLELY on the basis of the following passage.

The achievement of good human relations is essential if a business office is to produce at top efficiency and is to be a pleasant place in which to work. All office workers plan an important role in handling problems in human relations. They should, therefore, strive to acquire the understanding, tactfulness, and awareness necessary to deal effectively with actual office situations involving co-workers on all levels. Only in this way can they truly become responsible, interested, cooperative, and helpful members of the staff.

20. The selection implies that the MOST important value of good human relations in an office is to develop

    A. efficiency
    B. cooperativeness
    C. tact
    D. pleasantness and efficiency

21. Office workers should acquire understanding in dealing with

    A. co-workers
    B. subordinates
    C. superiors
    D. all members of the staff

22. The selection indicates that a highly competent secretary who is also very argumentative is meeting office requirements   22._____

    A. wholly
    B. partly
    C. slightly
    D. not at all

Questions 23-25.

DIRECTIONS: Questions 23 through 25 are to be answered SOLELY on the basis of the following passage.

It is common knowledge that ability to do a particular job and performance on the job do not always go hand in hand. Persons with great potential abilities sometimes fall down on the job because of laziness or lack of interest in the job, while persons with mediocre talents have often achieved excellent results through their industry and their loyalty to the interests of their employers. It is clear; therefore, that in a balanced personnel program, measures of employee ability need to be supplemented by measures of employee performance, for the final test of any employee is his performance on the job.

23. The MOST accurate of the following statements, on the basis of the above paragraph, is that   23._____

    A. employees who lack ability are usually not industrious
    B. an employee's attitudes are more important than his abilities
    C. mediocre employees who are interested in their work are preferable to employees who possess great ability
    D. superior capacity for performance should be supplemented with proper attitudes

24. On the basis of the above paragraph, the employee of most value to his employer is NOT necessarily the one who   24._____

    A. best understands the significance of his duties
    B. achieves excellent results
    C. possesses the greatest talents
    D. produces the greatest amount of work

25. According to the above paragraph, an employee's efficiency is BEST determined by an   25._____

    A. appraisal of his interest in his work
    B. evaluation of the work performed by him
    C. appraisal of his loyalty to his employer
    D. evaluation of his potential ability to perform his work

KEY (CORRECT ANSWERS)

1. B
2. A
3. C
4. C
5. A

6. D
7. A
8. C
9. D
10. B

11. C
12. A
13. D
14. D
15. B

16. C
17. C
18. B
19. D
20. D

21. D
22. B
23. D
24. C
25. B

TEST 3

Questions 1-8.

DIRECTIONS: Questions 1 through 8 are to be answered SOLELY on the basis of the following information and directions.

Assume that you are a clerk in a city agency. Your supervisor has asked you to classify each of the accidents that happened to employees in the agency into the following five categories:

    A. An accident that occurred in the period from January through June, between 9 A.M. and 12 Noon, that was the result of carelessness on the part of the injured employee, that caused the employee to lose less than seven working hours, that happened to an employee who was 40 years of age or over, and who was employed in the agency for less than three years;

    B. An accident that occurred in the period from July through December, after 1 P.M., that was the result of unsafe conditions, that caused the injured employee to lose less than seven working hours, that happened to an employee who was 40 years of age or over, and who was employed in the agency for three years or more;

    C. An accident that occurred in the period from January through June, after 1 P.M., that was the result of carelessness on the part of the injured employee, that caused the injured employee to lose seven or more working hours, that happened to an employee who was less than 40 years old, and who was employed in the agency for three years or more;

    D. An accident that occurred in the period from July through December, between 9 A.M. and 12 Noon, that was the result of unsafe conditions, that caused the injured employee to lose seven or more working hours, that happened to an employee who was less than 40 years old, and who was employed in the agency for less than three years;

    E. Accidents that cannot be classified in any of the foregoing groups. NOTE: In classifying these accidents, an employee's age and length of service are computed as of the date of accident. In all cases, it is to be assumed that each employee has been employed continuously in city service, and that each employee works seven hours a day, from 9 A.M. to 5 P.M., with lunch from 12 Noon to 1 P.M. In each question, consider only the information which will assist you in classifying the accident. Any information which is of no assistance in classifying an accident should not be considered.

1. The unsafe condition of the stairs in the building caused Miss Perkins to have an accident on October 14, 2003 at 4 P.M. When she returned to work the following day at 1 P.M., Miss Perkins said that the accident was the first one that had occurred to her in her ten years of employment with the agency. She was born on April 27, 1962.   1.____

2. On the day after she completed her six-month probationary period of employment with the agency, Miss Green, who had been considered a careful worker by her supervisor, injured her left foot in an accident caused by her own carelessness. She went home immediately after the accident, which occurred at 10 A.M., March 19, 2004, but returned to work at the regular time on the following morning. Miss Green was born July 12, 1963 in New York City.   2.____

3. The unsafe condition of a duplicating machine caused Mr. Martin to injure himself in an accident on September 8, 2006 at 2 P.M. As a result of the accident, he was unable to work the remainder of the day, but returned to his office ready for work on the following morning. Mr. Martin, who has been working for the agency since April 1, 2003, was born in St. Louis on February 1, 1968.

3.___

4. Mr. Smith was hospitalized for two weeks because of a back injury resulted from an accident on the morning of November 16, 2006. Investigation of the accident revealed that it was caused by the unsafe condition of the floor on which Mr. Smith had been walking. Mr. Smith, who is an accountant, has been anemployee of the agency since March 1, 2004, and was born in Ohio on June 10, 1968.

4.___

5. Mr. Allen cut his right hand because he was careless in operating a multilith machine. Mr. Allen, who was 33 years old when the accident took place, has been employed by the agency since August 17, 1992. The accident, which occurred on January 26, 2006, at 2 P.M., caused Mr. Allen to be absent from work for the rest of the day. He was able to return to work the next morning.

5.___

6. Mr. Rand, who is a college graduate, was born on December, 28, 1967, and has been working for the agency since January 7, 2002. On Monday, April 25, 2005, at 2 P.M., his carelessness in operating a duplicating machine caused him to have an accident and to be sent home from work immediately. Fortunately, he was able to return to work at his regular time on the following Wednesday.

6.___

7. Because he was careless in running down a flight of stairs, Mr. Brown fell, bruising his right hand. Although the accident occurred shortly after he arrived for work on the morning of May 22, 2006, he was unable to resume work until 3 P.M. that day. Mr. Brown was born on August 15, 1955, and began working for the agency on September 12, 2003, as a clerk, at a salary of $22,750 per annum.

7.___

8. On December 5, 2005, four weeks after he had begun working for the agency, the unsafe condition of an automatic stapling machine caused Mr. Thomas to injure himself in an accident. Mr. Thomas, who was born on May 19,1975, lost three working days because of the accident, which occurred at 11:45 A.M.

8.___

Questions 9-10.

DIRECTIONS: Questions 9 and 10 are to be answered SOLELY on the basis of the following paragraph.

An impending reorganization within an agency will mean loss by transfer of several professional staff members from the personnel division. The division chief is asked to designate the persons to be transferred. After reviewing the implications of this reduction of staff with his assistant, the division chief discusses the matter at a staff meeting. He adopts the recommendations of several staff members to have volunteers make up the required reduction.

9. The decision to permit personnel to volunteer for transfer is

    A. *poor;* it is not likely that the members of a division are of equal value to the division chief
    B. *good;* dissatisfied members will probably be more productive elsewhere
    C. *poor;* the division chief has abdicated his responsibility to carry out the order given to him
    D. *good;* morale among remaining staff is likely to improve in a more cohesive framework

10. Suppose that one of the volunteers is a recently appointed employee who has completed his probationary period acceptably, but whose attitude toward division operations and agency administration tends to be rather negative and sometimes even abrasive. Because of his lack of commitment to the division, his transfer is recommended. If the transfer is approved, the division chief should, prior to the transfer,

    A. discuss with the staff the importance of commitment to the work of the agency and its relationship with job satisfaction
    B. refrain from any discussion of attitude with the employee
    C. discuss with the employee his concern about the employee's attitude
    D. avoid mention of attitude in the evaluation appraisal prepared for the receiving division chief

Questions 11-16.

DIRECTIONS: Questions 11 through 16 are to be answered SOLELY on the basis of the following paragraph.

Methods of administration of office activities, much of which consists of providing information and *know-how* needed to coordinate both activities within that particular office and other offices, have been among the last to come under the spotlight of management analysis. Progress has been rapid during the past decade, however, and is now accelerating at such a pace that an *information revolution* in office management appears to be in the making. Although triggered by technological breakthroughs in electronic computers and other giant steps in mechanization, this information revolution must be attributed to underlying forces, such as the increased complexity of both governmental and private enterprise, and ever-keener competition. Size, diversification, specialization of function, and decentralization are among the forces which make coordination of activities both more imperative and more difficult. Increased competition, both domestic and international, leaves little margin for error in managerial decisions. Several developments during recent years indicate an evolving pattern. In 1960, the American Management Association expanded the scope of its activities and changed the name of its Office Management Division to Administrative Services Division. Also in 1960, the magazine *Office Management* merged with the magazine *American Business*, and this new publication was named *Administrative Management*.

11. A REASONABLE inference that can be made from the information in the above paragraph is that an important role of the office manager today is to

    A. work toward specialization of functions performed by his subordinates
    B. inform and train subordinates regarding any new developments in computer technology and mechanization
    C. assist the professional management analysts with the management analysis work in the organization
    D. supply information that can be used to help coordinate and manage the other activities of the organization

12. An IMPORTANT reason for the *information revolution* that has been taking place in office management is the

    A. advance made in management analysis in the past decade
    B. technological breakthrough in electronic computers and mechanization
    C. more competitive and complicated nature of private business and government
    D. increased efficiency of office management techniques in the past ten years

13. According to the above paragraph, specialization of function in an organization is MOST likely to result in

    A. the elimination of errors in managerial decisions
    B. greater need to coordinate activities
    C. more competition with other organizations, both domestic and international
    D. a need for office managers with greater flexibility

14. The word *evolving*, as used in the third from last sentence in the above paragraph, means MOST NEARLY

    A. developing by gradual changes
    B. passing on to others
    C. occurring periodically
    D. breaking up into separate, constituent parts

15. Of the following, the MOST reasonable implication of the changes in names mentioned in the last part of the above paragraph is that these groups are attempting to

    A. professionalize the field of office management and the title of Office Manager
    B. combine two publications into one because of the increased costs of labor and materials
    C. adjust to the fact that the field of office management is broadening
    D. appeal to the top managerial people rather than the office management people in business and government

16. According to the above paragraph, intense competition among domestic and international enterprises makes it MOST important for an organization's managerial staff to

    A. coordinate and administer office activities with other activities in the organization
    B. make as few errors in decision-making as possible
    C. concentrate on decentralization and reduction of size of the individual divisions of the organization
    D. restrict decision-making only to top management officials

Questions 17-21.

DIRECTIONS: Questions 17 through 21 are to be answered SOLELY on the basis of the following passage.

For some office workers, it is useful to be familiar with the four main classes of domestic mail; for others, it is essential. Each class has a different rate of postage, and some have requirements concerning wrapping, sealing, or special information to be placed on the package. First class mail, the class which may not be opened for postal inspection, includes letters, postcards, business reply cards, and other kinds of written matter. There are different rates for some of the kinds of cards which can be sent by first class mail. The maximum weight for an item sent by first class mail is 70 pounds. An item which is not letter size should be marked *First Class* on all sides. Although office workers most often come into contact with first class mail, they may find it helpful to know something about the other classes. Second class mail is generally used for mailing newspapers and magazines. Publishers of these articles must meet certain U.S. Postal Service requirements in order to obtain a permit to use second class mailing rates. Third class mail, which must weigh less than 1 pound, includes printed materials and merchandise parcels. There are two rate structures for this class - a single piece rate and a bulk rate. Fourth class mail, also known as parcel post, includes packages weighing from one to 40 pounds. For more information about these classes of mail and the actual mailing rates, contact your local post office.

17. According to this passage, first class mail is the *only* class which

   A. has a limit on the maximum weight of an item
   B. has different rates for items within the class
   C. may not be opened for postal inspection
   D. should be used by office workers

18. According to this passage, the one of the following items which may CORRECTLY be sent by fourth class mail is a

   A. magazine weighing one-half pound
   B. package weighing one-half pound
   C. package weighing two pounds
   D. postcard

19. According to this passage, there are different postage rates for

   A. a newspaper sent by second class mail and a magazine sent by second class mail
   B. each of the classes of mail
   C. each pound of fourth class mail
   D. printed material sent by third class mail and merchandise parcels sent by third class mail

20. In order to send a newspaper by second class mail, a publisher MUST

   A. have met certain postal requirements and obtained a permit
   B. indicate whether he wants to use the single piece or the bulk rate
   C. make certain that the newspaper weighs less than one pound
   D. mark the newspaper *Second Class* on the top and bottom of the wrapper

21. Of the following types of information, the one which is NOT mentioned in the passage is the

    A. class of mail to which parcel post belongs
    B. kinds of items which can be sent by each class of mail
    C. maximum weight for an item sent by fourth class mail
    D. postage rate for each of the four classes of mail

Questions 22-25.

DIRECTIONS: Questions 22 through 25 are to be answered SOLELY on the basis of the following paragraph.

A standard comprises characteristics attached to an aspect of a process or product by which it can be evaluated. Standardization is the development and adoption of standards. When they are formulated, standards are not usually the product of a single person, but represent the thoughts and ideas of a group, leavened with the knowledge and information which are currently available. Standards which do not meet certain basic requirements become a hindrance rather than an aid to progress. Standards must not only be correct, accurate, and precise in requiring no more and no less than what is needed for satisfactory results, but they must also be workable in the sense that their usefulness is not nullified by external conditions. Standards should also be acceptable to the people who use them. If they are not acceptable, they cannot be considered to be satisfactory, although they may possess all the other essential characteristics.

22. According to the above paragraph, a processing standard that requires the use of materials that cannot be procured is MOST likely to be

    A. incomplete   B. unworkable
    C. inaccurate   D. unacceptable

23. According to the above paragraph, the construction of standards to which the performance of job duties should conform is MOST often

    A. the work of the people responsible for seeing that the duties are properly performed
    B. accomplished by the person who is best informed about the functions involved
    C. the responsibility of the people who are to apply them
    D. attributable to the efforts of various informed persons

24. According to the above paragraph, when standards call for finer tolerances than those essential to the conduct of successful production operations, the effect of the standards on the improvement of production operations is

    A. negative   B. negligible
    C. nullified   D. beneficial

25. The one of the following which is the MOST suitable title for the above paragraph is

    A. THE EVALUATION OF FORMULATED STANDARDS
    B. THE ATTRIBUTES OF SATISFACTORY STANDARDS
    C. THE ADOPTION OF ACCEPTABLE STANDARDS
    D. THE USE OF PROCESS OR PRODUCT STANDARDS

KEY (CORRECT ANSWERS)

1. B
2. A
3. E
4. D
5. E

6. C
7. A
8. D
9. A
10. C

11. D
12. C
13. B
14. A
15. C

16. B
17. C
18. C
19. B
20. A

21. D
22. C
23. D
24. A
25. B

INTERPRETING STATISTICAL DATA GRAPHS, CHARTS AND TABLES

EXAMINATION SECTION

TEST 1

DIRECTIONS: Each question or incomplete statement is followed by several suggested answers or completions. Select the one that BEST answers the question or completes the statement. *PRINT THE LETTER OF THE CORRECT ANSWER IN THE SPACE AT THE RIGHT.*

Questions 1-8.

DIRECTIONS: Questions 1 through 8 are to be answered SOLELY on the basis of the information and chart given below.

The following chart shows expenses in five selected categories for a one-year period expressed as percentages of these same expenses during the previous year. The chart compares two different offices. In Office T (represented by ☐) a cost reduction program has been tested for the past year. The other office, Office Q (represented by ▨) served as a control, in that no special effort was made to reduce costs during the past year.

RESULTS OF OFFICE COST REDUCTION PROGRAM

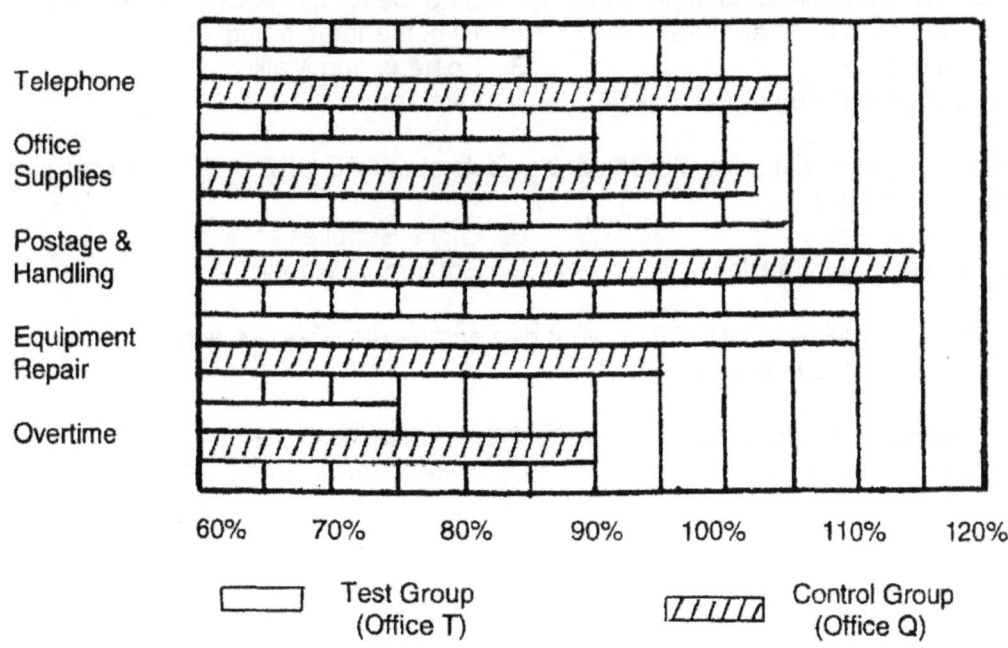

Expenses of Test and Control Groups for 2019
Expressed as Percentages of Same Expenses for 2018

1. In Office T, which category of expenses showed the GREATEST percentage reduction from 2018 to 2019?
    A. Telephone
    B. Office Supplies
    C. Postage and Mailing
    D. Overtime

2. In which expense category did Office T show the BEST results in percentage terms when compared to Office Q?
    A. Telephone
    B. Office Supplies
    C. Postage and Mailing
    D. Overtime

3. According to the above chart, the cost reduction program was LEAST effective for the expense category of
    A. Office Supplies
    B. Postage and Mailing
    C. Equipment Repair
    D. Overtime

4. Office T's telephone costs went down during 2019 by APPROXIMATELY how many percentage points?
    A. 15   B. 20   C. 85   D. 105

5. Which of the following changes occurred in expenses for Office Supplies in Office Q in the year 2019 as compared with the year 2018?
    They
    A. *increased* by more than 100%
    B. *remained* the same
    C. *decreased* by a few percentage points
    D. *increased* by a few percentage points

6. For which of the following expense categories do the results in Office T and the results in Office Q differ MOST NEARLY by 10 percentage points?
    A. Telephone
    B. Postage and Mailing
    C. Equipment Repair
    D. Overtime

7. In which expense category did Office Q's costs show the GREATEST percentage increase in 2019?
    A. Telephone
    B. Office Supplies
    C. Postage and Mailing
    D. Equipment Repair

8. In Office T, by APPROXIMATELY what percentage did overtime expense change during the past year?
    It
    A. *increased* by 15%
    B. *increased* by 75%
    C. *decreased* by 10%
    D. *decreased* by 25%

3 (#1)

KEY (CORRECT ANSWERS)

1. D 5. D
2. A 6. B
3. C 7. C
4. A 8. D

TEST 2

DIRECTIONS: Each question or incomplete statement is followed by several suggested answers or completions. Select the one that BEST answers the question or completes the statement. *PRINT THE LETTER OF THE CORRECT ANSWER IN THE SPACE AT THE RIGHT.*

Questions 1-7.

DIRECTIONS: Questions 1 through 7 are to be answered SOLELY on the basis of the information contained in the following graph which relates to the work of a public agency.

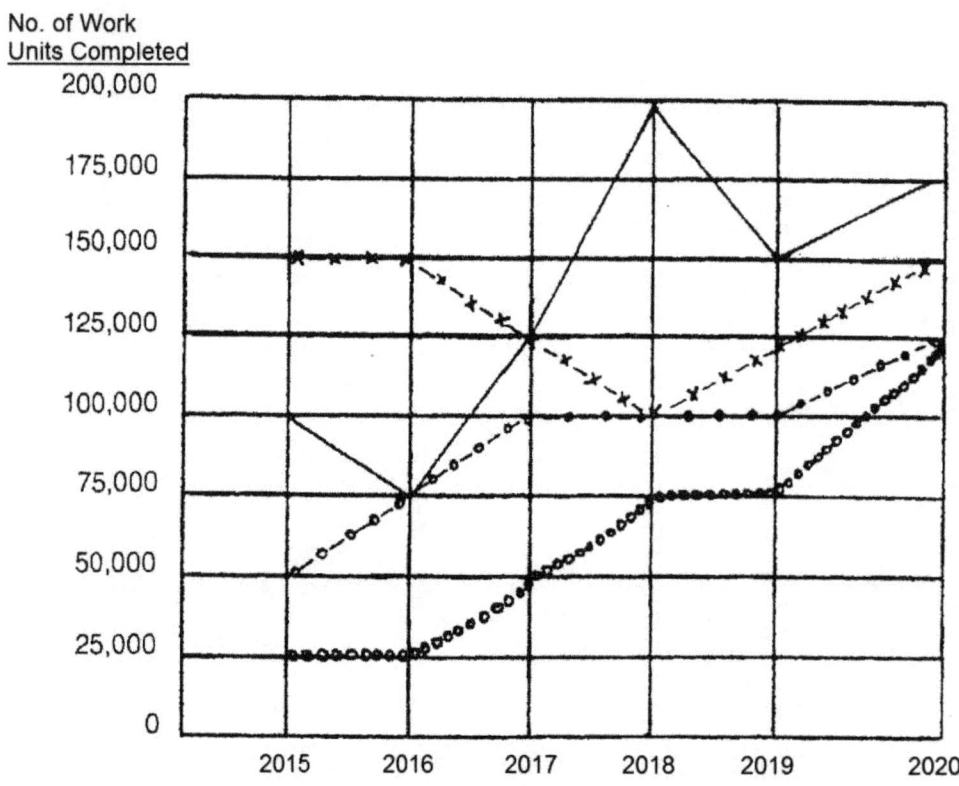

Units of each type of work completed by a public agency from 2015 to 2020.

Letters Written ───────
Documents Filed –x-x-x-x-x-x

Applications Processed -0-0-0-0-0
Inspections Made 0000000000000

1. The year for which the number of units of one type of work completed was less than it was for the previous year while the number of each of the other types of work completed was more than it was for the previous year was
   A. 2016   B. 2017   C. 2018   D. 2019

    1.____

2. The number of letters written exceeded the number of applications processed by the same amount in _____ of the years.
   A. two   B. three   C. four   D. five

    2.____

146

2 (#2)

3. The year in which the number of each type of work completed was GREATER than in the preceding year was
   A. 2017   B. 2018   C. 2019   D. 2020

   3._____

4. The number of applications processed and the number of documents filed were the SAME in
   A. 2016   B. 2017   C. 2018   D. 2019

   4._____

5. The TOTAL number of units of work completed by the agency
   A. increased in each year after 2015
   B. decreased from the prior year in two of the years after 2015
   C. was the same in two successive years from 2015 to 2020
   D. was less in 2015 than in any of the following years

   5._____

6. For the year in which the number of letters written was twice as high as it was in 2015, the number of documents filed was _____ it was in 2015.
   A. the same as   B. two-thirds of what
   C. five-sixths of what   D. one and one-half times what

   6._____

7. The variable which was the MOST stable during the period 2015 through 2020 was
   A. Inspections Made   B. Letters Written
   C. Documents Filed   D. Applications Processed

   7._____

KEY (CORRECT ANSWERS)

1.	B	5.	C
2.	B	6.	B
3.	D	7.	D
4.	C		

TEST 3

DIRECTIONS: Each question or incomplete statement is followed by several suggested answers or completions. Select the one that BEST answers the question or completes the statement. *PRINT THE LETTER OF THE CORRECT ANSWER IN THE SPACE AT THE RIGHT.*

Questions 1-10.

DIRECTIONS: Questions 1 through 10 are to be answered SOLELY on the basis of the REPORT OF TELEPHONE CALLS table given below.

			No. of Incoming Calls In		No. of Long Distance Calls in		
Dept.	No. of Stations	No. of Employees	2019	2020	2019	2020	No. of Divisions
I	11	40	3421	4292	72	54	5
II	36	330	10392	10191	75	78	18
III	53	250	85243	85084	103	98	8
IV	24	60	9675	10123	82	85	6
V	13	30	5208	5492	54	48	6
VI	25	35	7472	8109	86	90	5
VII	37	195	11412	11299	68	72	11
VIII	36	54	8467	8674	59	68	4
IX	163	306	294321	289968	289	321	13
X	40	83	9588	8266	93	89	5
XI	24	68	7867	7433	86	87	13
XII	50	248	10039	10208	101	95	30
XIII	10	230	7550	6941	28	21	10
XVI	25	103	14281	14392	48	40	5
XV	19	230	8475	206	38	43	8
XVI	22	45	4684	5584	39	48	10
XVII	41	58	10102	9677	49	52	6
XVIII	82	106	106242	105889	128	132	10
XIX	6	13	2649	2498	35	29	2
XX	16	30	1395	1468	78	90	2

1. The department which had more than 106,000 incoming calls in 2019 but fewer than 250,000 is
   A. II   B. IX   C. XVIII   D. III

   1.____

2. The department which has fewer than 8 divisions and more than 100 but fewer than 300 employees is
   A. VII   B. XIV   C. XV   D. XVIII

   2.____

3. The department which had an increase in 2020 over 2019 in the number of both incoming and long distance calls but had an increase in long distance calls of not more than 3 was
   A. IV   B. VI   C. XVII   D. XVIII

   3.____

2 (#3)

4. The department which had a decrease in the number of incoming calls in 2020 as compared to 2019 and has not less than 6 nor more than 7 divisions is
   A. IV   B. V   C. XVII   D. III

   4.____

5. The department which has more than 7 divisions and more than 200 employees but fewer than 19 stations is
   A. XV   B. III   C. XX   D. XIII

   5.____

6. The department having more than 10 divisions and fewer than 36 stations, which had an increase in long distance calls in 2020 over 2019, is
   A. XI   B. VII   C. XVI   D. XVIII

   6.____

7. The department which in 2020 had at least 7,250 incoming calls and a decrease in long distance calls from 2019 and has more than 50 stations is
   A. IX   B. XII   C. XVIII   D. III

   7.____

8. The department which has fewer than 25 stations, fewer than 100 employees, 10 or more divisions, and showed an increase of at least 9 long distance calls in 2020 over 2019 is
   A. IX   B. XVI   C. XX   D. XIII

   8.____

9. The department which has more than 50 but fewer than 125 employees and had more than 5,000 incoming calls in 2019 but not more than 10,000, and more than 60 long distance calls in 2020 but not more than 85, and has more than 24 stations is
   A. VIII   B. XIV   C. IV   D. XI

   9.____

10. If the number of departments showing an increase in long distance calls in 2020 over 1999 exceeds the number showing a decrease in long distance calls in the same period, select the Roman numeral indicating the department having less than one station for each 10 employees, provided not more than 8 divisions are served by that department.
    If the number of departments showing an increase in long distance calls in 2020 over 2019 does not exceed the number showing a decrease in long distance calls in the same period, select the Roman numeral indicating the department having the SMALLEST number of incoming calls in 2020.
    A. III   B. XIII   C. XV   D. XX

    10.____

KEY (CORRECT ANSWERS)

1.	C	6.	A
2.	B	7.	D
3.	A	8.	B
4.	C	9.	A
5.	D	10.	C

TEST 4

DIRECTIONS: Each question or incomplete statement is followed by several suggested answers or completions. Select the one that BEST answers the question or completes the statement. *PRINT THE LETTER OF THE CORRECT ANSWER IN THE SPACE AT THE RIGHT.*

Questions 1-6.

DIRECTIONS: Questions 1 through 6 are to be answered SOLELY on the basis of the information given in the following chart. This chart shows the results of a study made of the tasks performed by a stenographer during one day. Included in the chart are the time at which she started a certain task and, under the particular heading, the amount of time, in minutes, she took to complete the task, and explanations of telephone calls and miscellaneous activities. NOTE: The time spent at lunch should not be included in any of your calculations.

	PAMELA JOB STUDY						
NAME: Pamela Donald							DATE: 9/26
JOB TITLE: Stenographer							
DIVISION: Stenographic Pool							

Time of Start of Task	TASKS PERFORMED						Explanations of Telephone Calls and Miscellaneous Activities
	Taking Dictation	Typing	Filing	Telephone Work	Handling Mail	Misc. Activities	
9:00					22		
9:22						13	Picking up supplies
9:35						15	Cleaning typewriter
9:50	11						
10:01		30					
10:31				8			Call to Agency A
10:39	12						
10:51			10				
11:01				7			Call from Agency B
11:08		30					
11:38	10						
11:48				12			Call from Agency C
12:00	L U N C H						
1:00					28		
1:28	13						
1:41-2:13		32		12			Call to Agency B
X			15				
Y		50					
3:30	10						
3:40			21				
4:01				9			Call from Agency A
4:10	35						
4:45		9					
4:54						6	Cleaning up desk

151

2 (#4)

SAMPLE QUESTION:
The total amount of time spent on miscellaneous activities in the morning is exactly equal to the total amount of time spent
- A. filing in the morning
- B. handling mail in the afternoon
- C. miscellaneous activities in the afternoon
- D. handling mail in the morning

Explanation of answer to sample question:
The total amount of time spent on miscellaneous activities in the morning equals 28 minutes (13 minutes for picking up supplies plus 15 minutes for cleaning the typewriter); and since it takes 28 minutes to handle mail in the afternoon, the answer is B.

1. The time labeled Y at which the stenographer started a typing assignment was
    A. 2:15   B. 2:25   C. 2:40   D. 2:50

2. The ratio of time spent on all incoming calls to time spent on all outgoing calls for the day was
    A. 5:7   B. 5:12   C. 7:5   D. 7:12

3. Of the following combinations of tasks, which ones take up exactly 80% of the total time spent on Tasks Performed during the day?
    A. Typing, Filing, Telephone Work, Handling Mail
    B. Taking Dictation, Filing, and Miscellaneous Activities
    C. Taking Dictation, Typing, Handling Mail, and Miscellaneous Activities
    D. Taking Dictation, Typing, Filing, and Telephone Work

4. The total amount of time spent transcribing or typing work is how much MORE than the total amount of time spent in taking dictation?
    A. 55 minutes   B. 1 hour
    C. 1 hour 10 minutes   D. 1 hour 25 minutes

5. The GREATEST number of shifts in activities occurred between the times of
    A. 9:00 A.M. and 10:31 A.M.   B. 9:35 A.M. and 11:01 A.M.
    C. 10:31 A.M. and 12:00 Noon   D. 3:30 P.M. and 5:00 P.M.

6. The total amount of time spent on Taking Dictation in the morning plus the total amount of time spent on Filing in the afternoon is exactly EQUAL to the total amount of time spent on
    A. Typing in the afternoon minus the total amount of time spent on Telephone Work in the afternoon
    B. Typing in the morning plus the total amount of time spent on Miscellaneous Activities
    C. Dictation in the afternoon plus the total amount of time spent on Filing in the morning
    D. Typing in the afternoon minus the total amount of time spent in Handling Mail in the morning

KEY (CORRECT ANSWERS)

1. C
2. C
3. D
4. B
5. C
6. D

TEST 5

DIRECTIONS: Each question or incomplete statement is followed by several suggested answers or completions. Select the one that BEST answers the question or completes the statement. *PRINT THE LETTER OF THE CORRECT ANSWER IN THE SPACE AT THE RIGHT.*

Questions 1-8.

DIRECTIONS: Questions 1 through 8 are to be answered SOLELY on the basis of the information given in the following table.

	Bronx		Brooklyn		Manhattan		Queens		Richmond	
	May	June	May	June	May	June	May	June	May	June
Number of Clerks in Office Assigned To Issue Applications for Licenses	3	4	6	8	6	8	3	5	2	4
Number of Licenses Issued	950	1010	1620	1940	1705	2025	895	1250	685	975
Amount Collected in License Fees	$42,400	$52,100	$77,600	$94,500	$83,700	$98,800	$39,300	$65,500	$30,600	$48,200
Number of Inspectors	4	5	6	7	7	8	4	5	2	4
Number of Inspections Made	420	450	630	710	690	740	400	580	320	440
Number of Violations Found As a Result of Inspections	211	153	352	378	320	385	256	304	105	247

1. Of the following statements, the one which is NOT accurate on the basis of an inspection of the information contained in the table is that, for each office, the increase from May to June in the number of
    A. inspectors was accompanied by an increase in the number of inspections made
    B. licenses issued was accompanied by an increase in the amount collected in license fees
    C. inspections made was accompanied by an increase in the number of violations found
    D. licenses issued was accompanied by an increase in the number of clerks assigned to issue applications for licenses

1.____

2. The TOTAL number of licenses issued by all five offices in the Division in May was
    A. 4,800   B. 5,855   C. 6,865   D. 7,200

2.____

3. The total number of inspectors in all five borough offices in June exceeded the number in May by MOST NEARLY
    A. 21%   B. 26%   C. 55%   D. 70%

3.____

2 (#5)

4. In the month of June, the number of violations found per inspection made was the HIGHEST in
    A. Brooklyn   B. Manhattan   C. Queens   D. Richmond

    4.____

5. In the month of May, the average number of inspections made by an inspector in the Bronx was the same as the average number of inspections made by an inspector in
    A. Brooklyn   B. Manhattan   C. Queens   D. Richmond

    5.____

6. Assume that in June all of the inspectors in the Division spent 7 hours a day making inspections on each of the 21 working days in the month.
   Then the average amount of time that an inspector in the Manhattan office spent on an inspection that month was MOST NEARLY
    A. 2 hours
    B. 1 hour and 35 minutes
    C. 1 hour and 3 minutes
    D. 38 minutes

    6.____

7. If an average fine of $100 was imposed for a violation found by the Division, what was the TOTAL amount in fines imposed for all the violations found by the Division in May?
    A. $124,400   B. $133,500   C. $146,700   D. $267,000

    7.____

8. Assume that the amount collected in license fees by the entire Division in May was 80 percent of the amount collected by the entire Division in April.
   How much was collected by the entire Division in April?
    A. $218,880   B. $328,320   C. $342,000   D. $410,400

    8.____

KEY (CORRECT ANSWERS)

1.	C	5.	A
2.	B	6.	B
3.	B	7.	A
4.	D	8.	C

TEST 6

DIRECTIONS: Each question or incomplete statement is followed by several suggested answers or completions. Select the one that BEST answers the question or completes the statement. *PRINT THE LETTER OF THE CORRECT ANSWER IN THE SPACE AT THE RIGHT.*

Questions 1-8.

DIRECTIONS: Questions 1 through 8 are to be answered SOLELY on the basis of the information contained in the chart and table shown below, which relate to Bureau X in a certain public agency. The chart shows the percentage of the bureau's annual expenditures spent on equipment, supplies, and salaries for each of the years 2016-2020. The table shows the bureau's annual expenditures for each of the years 2016-2020.

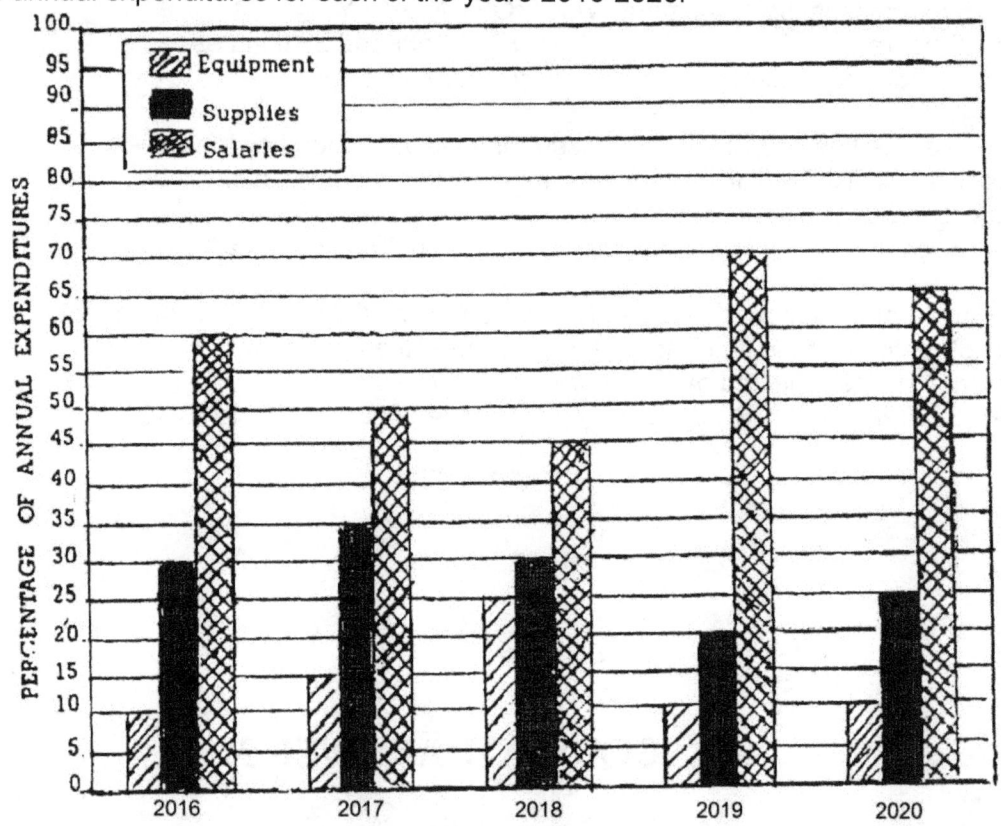

The bureau's annual expenditures for the years 2016-2020 are shown in the following table:

YEAR	EXPENDITURES
2016	$8,000,000
2017	$12,000,000
2018	$15,000,000
2019	$10,000,000
2020	$12,000,000

2 (#6)

Equipment, supplies, and salaries were the only three categories for which the bureau spent money.
Candidates may find it useful to arrange their computations on their scratch paper in an orderly manner since the correct computations for one question may also be helpful in answering another question.

1. The information contained in the chart and table is sufficient to determine the
   A. average annual salary of an employee in the bureau in 2017
   B. decrease in the amount of money spent on supplies in the bureau in 2016 from the amount spent in the preceding year
   C. changes between 2018 and 2019 in the prices of supplies bought by the bureau
   D. increase in the amount of money spent on salaries in the bureau in 2020 over the amount spent in the preceding year

2. If the percentage of expenditures for salaries in one year is added to the percentage of expenditures for equipment in that year, a total of two percentages for that year is obtained.
   The two years for which this total is the SAME are
   A. 2016 and 2018
   B. 2017 and 2019
   C. 2016 and 2019
   D. 2017 and 2020

3. Of the following, the year in which the bureau spent the GREATEST amount of money on supplies was
   A. 2020
   B. 2018
   C. 2016
   D. 2016

4. Of the following years, the one in which there was the GREATEST increase over the preceding year in the amount of money spent on salaries is
   A. 2019
   B. 2020
   C. 2016
   D. 2018

5. Of the bureau's expenditures for equipment in 2020, one-third was used for the purchase of mailroom equipment and the remainder was spent on miscellaneous office equipment.
   How much did the bureau spend on miscellaneous office equipment in 2020?
   A. $4,000,000
   B. $400,000
   C. $8,000,000
   D. $800,000

6. If there were 120 employees in the bureau in 2019, then the average annual salary paid to the employees in that year was MOST NEARLY
   A. $43,450
   B. $49,600
   C. $58,350
   D. $80,800

7. In 2018, the bureau had 125 employees.
   If 20 of the employees earned an average annual salary of $80,000, then the average salary of the other 105 employees was MOST NEARLY
   A. $49,000
   B. $64,000
   C. $41,000
   D. $54,000

8. Assume that the bureau estimated that the amount of money it would spend on supplies in 2021 would be the same as the amount it spent on that category in 2020. Similarly, the bureau estimated that the amount of money it would spend on equipment in 2021 would be the same as the amount it spent on that category in 2020. However, the bureau estimated that in 2021 the amount it would spend on salaries would be 10 percent higher than the amount it spent on that category in 2020.
The percentage of its annual expenditures that the bureau estimated it would spend on supplies in 2021 is MOST NEARLY
   A. 27.5%   B. 23.5%   C. 22.5%   D. 25%

8._____

KEY (CORRECT ANSWERS)

1. D   5. D
2. A   6. C
3. B   7. A
4. C   8. B

MAP READING
EXAMINATION SECTION
TEST 1

DIRECTIONS: Each question or incomplete statement is followed by several suggested answers or completions. Select the one that BEST answers the question or completes the Statement. *PRINT THE LETTER OF THE CORRECT ANSWER IN THE SPACE AT THE RIGHT.*

Questions 1-5.

DIRECTIONS: Questions 1 through 5 are to be answered SOLELY on the basis of the following information and map.

An employee may be required to assist civilians who seek travel directions or referral to city agencies and facilities.

The following is a map of part of a city, where several public offices and other institutions are located. Each of the squares represents one city block. Street names are as shown. If there is an arrow next to the street name, it means the street is one-way only in the direction of the arrow. If there is no arrow next to the street name, two-way traffic is allowed.

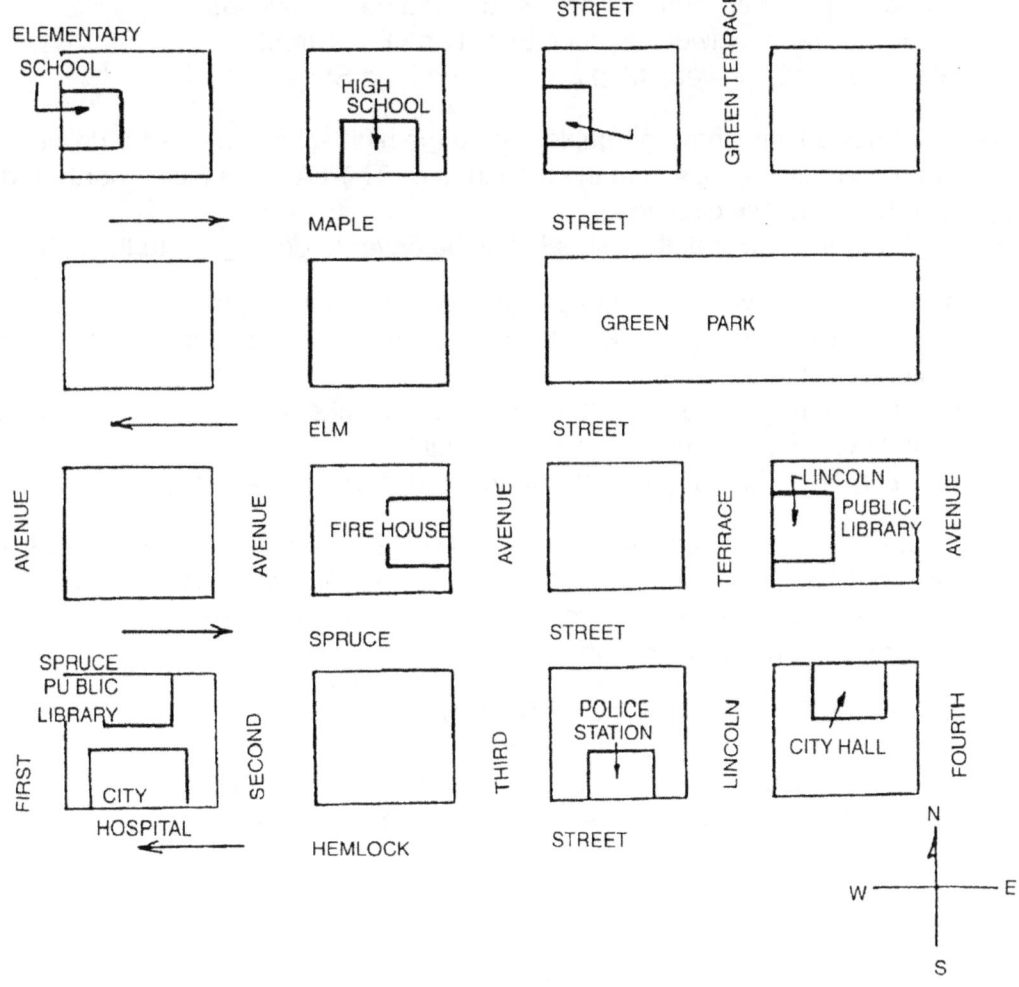

1. A woman whose handbag was stolen from her in Green Park asks a firefighter at the firehouse where to go to report the crime.
   The firefighter should tell the woman to go to the

   A. police station on Spruce Street
   B. police station on Hemlock Street
   C. city hall on Spruce Street
   D. city hall on Hemlock Street

2. A disabled senior citizen who lives on Green Terrace telephones the firehouse to ask which library is closest to her home.
   The firefighter should tell the senior citizen it is the

   A. Spruce Public Library on Lincoln Terrace
   B. Lincoln Public Library on Spruce Street
   C. Spruce Public Library on Spruce Street
   D. Lincoln Public Library on Lincoln Terrace

3. A woman calls the firehouse to ask for the exact location of City Hall.
   She should be told that it is on

   A. Hemlock Street, between Lincoln Terrace and Fourth Avenue
   B. Spruce Street, between Lincoln Terrace and Fourth Avenue
   C. Lincoln Terrace, between Spruce Street and Elm Street
   D. Green Terrace, between Maple Street and Pine Street

4. A delivery truck driver is having trouble finding the high school to make a delivery. The driver parks the truck across from the firehouse on Third Avenue facing north and goes into the firehouse to ask directions.
   In giving directions, the firefighter should tell the driver to go _____ to the school.

   A. north on Third Avenue to Pine Street and then make a right
   B. south on Third Avenue, make a left on Hemlock Street, and then make a right on Second Avenue
   C. north on Third Avenue, turn left on Elm Street, make a right on Second Avenue and go to Maple Street, then make another right
   D. north on Third Avenue to Maple Street, and then make a left

5. A man comes to the firehouse accompanied by his son and daughter. He wants to register his son in the high school and his daughter in the elementary school. He asks a firefighter which school is closest for him to walk to from the firehouse.
   The firefighter should tell the man that the

   A. high school is closer than the elementary school
   B. elementary school is closer than the high school
   C. elementary school and high school are the same distance away
   D. elementary school and high school are in opposite directions

Questions 6-8.

DIRECTIONS: Questions 6 through 8 are to be answered SOLELY on the basis of the following map and information. The flow of traffic is indicated by the arrows. If there is only one arrow shown, then traffic flows in the direction indicated by the arrow. If there are two arrows, then traffic flows in both directions. You must follow the flow of traffic

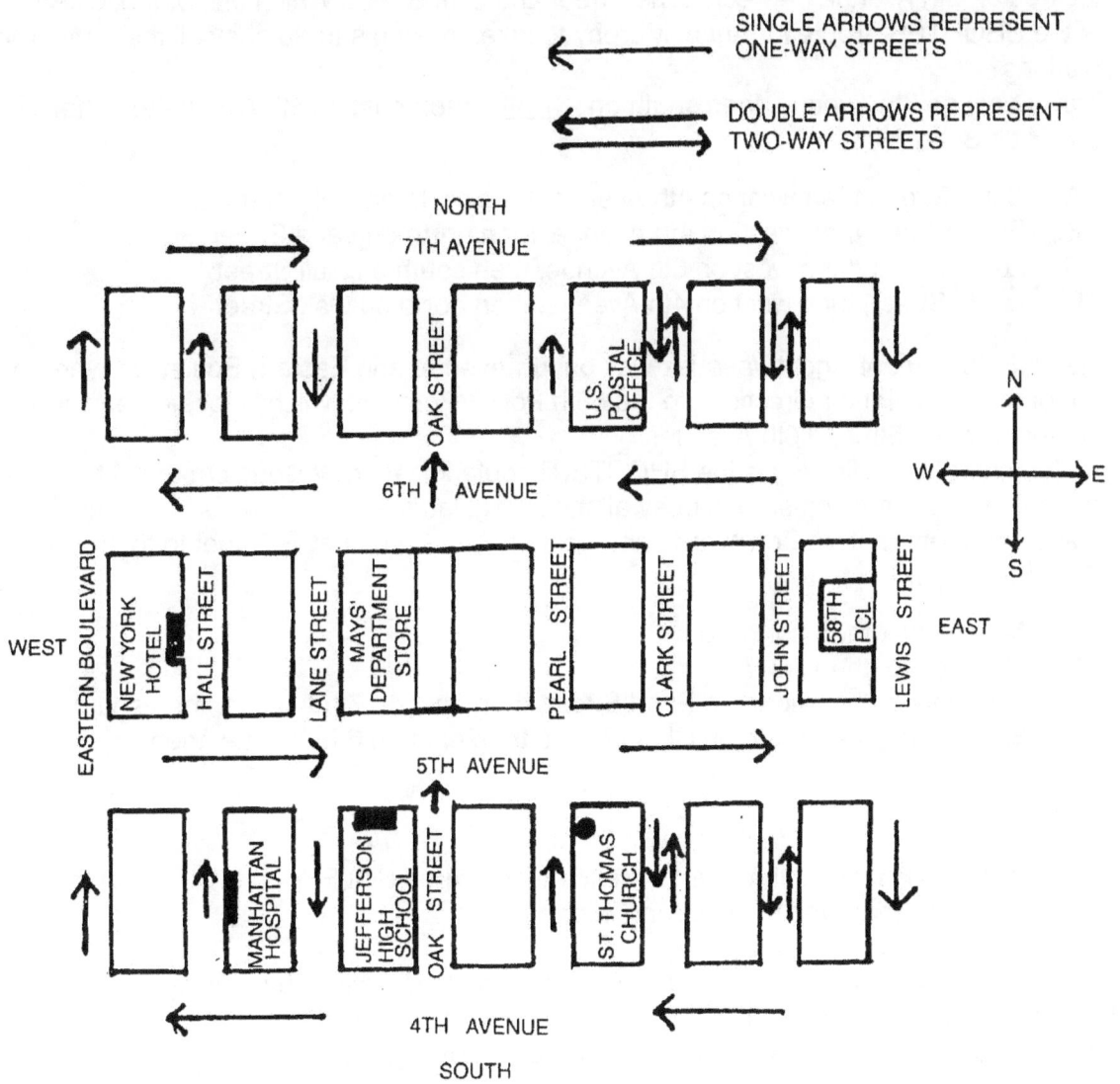

6. Traffic Enforcement Agent Fox was on foot patrol at John Street between 6th and 7th Avenues when a motorist driving southbound asked her for directions to the New York Hotel, which is located on Hall Street between 5th and 6th Avenues. Which one of the following is the SHORTEST route for Agent Fox to direct the motorist to take, making sure to obey all traffic regulations?
Travel _____ to the New York Hotel.

   A. north on John Street, then east on 7th Avenue, then north on Lewis Street, then west on 4th Avenue, then north on Eastern Boulevard, then east on 5th Avenue, then north on Hall Street
   B. south on John Street, then west on 6th Avenue, then south on Eastern Boulevard, then east on 5th Avenue, then north on Hall Street

6.____

C. south on John Street, then west on 6th Avenue, then south on Clark Street, then east on 4th Avenue, then north on Eastern Boulevard, then east on 5th Avenue, then north on Hall Street
D. south on John Street, then west on 4th Avenue, then north on Hall Street

7. Traffic Enforcement Agent Murphy is on motorized patrol on 7th Avenue between Oak Street and Pearl Street when Lt. Robertson radios him to go to Jefferson High School, located on 5th Avenue between Lane Street and Oak Street. Which one of the following is the SHORTEST route for Agent Murphy to take, making sure to obey all the traffic regulations?
Travel east on 7th Avenue, then south on _____, then east on 5th Avenue to Jefferson High School.

7._____

A. Clark Street, then west on 4th Avenue, then north on Hall Street
B. Pearl Street, then west on 4th Avenue, then north on Lane Street
C. Lewis Street, then west on 6th Avenue, then south on Hall Street
D. Lewis Street, then west on 4th Avenue, then north on Oak Street

8. Traffic Enforcement Agent Vasquez was on 4th Avenue and Eastern Boulevard when a motorist asked him for directions to the 58th Police Precinct, which is located on Lewis Street between 5th and 6th Avenues.
Which one of the following is the SHORTEST route for Agent Vasquez to direct the motorist to take, making sure to obey all traffic regulations.
Travel north on Eastern Boulevard, then east on _____ on Lewis Street to the 58th Police Precinct.

8._____

A. 5th Avenue, then north
B. 7th Avenue, then south
C. 6th Avenue, then north on Pearl Street, then east on 7th Avenue, then south
D. 5th Avenue, then north on Clark Street, then east on 6th Avenue, then south

Questions 9-13.

DIRECTIONS: Questions 9 through 13 are to be answered SOLELY on the basis of the following map and the following information.

Toll collectors answer motorists' questions concerning directions by reading a map of the metropolitan area. Although many alternate routes leading to destinations exist on the following map, you are to choose the MOST direct route of those given.

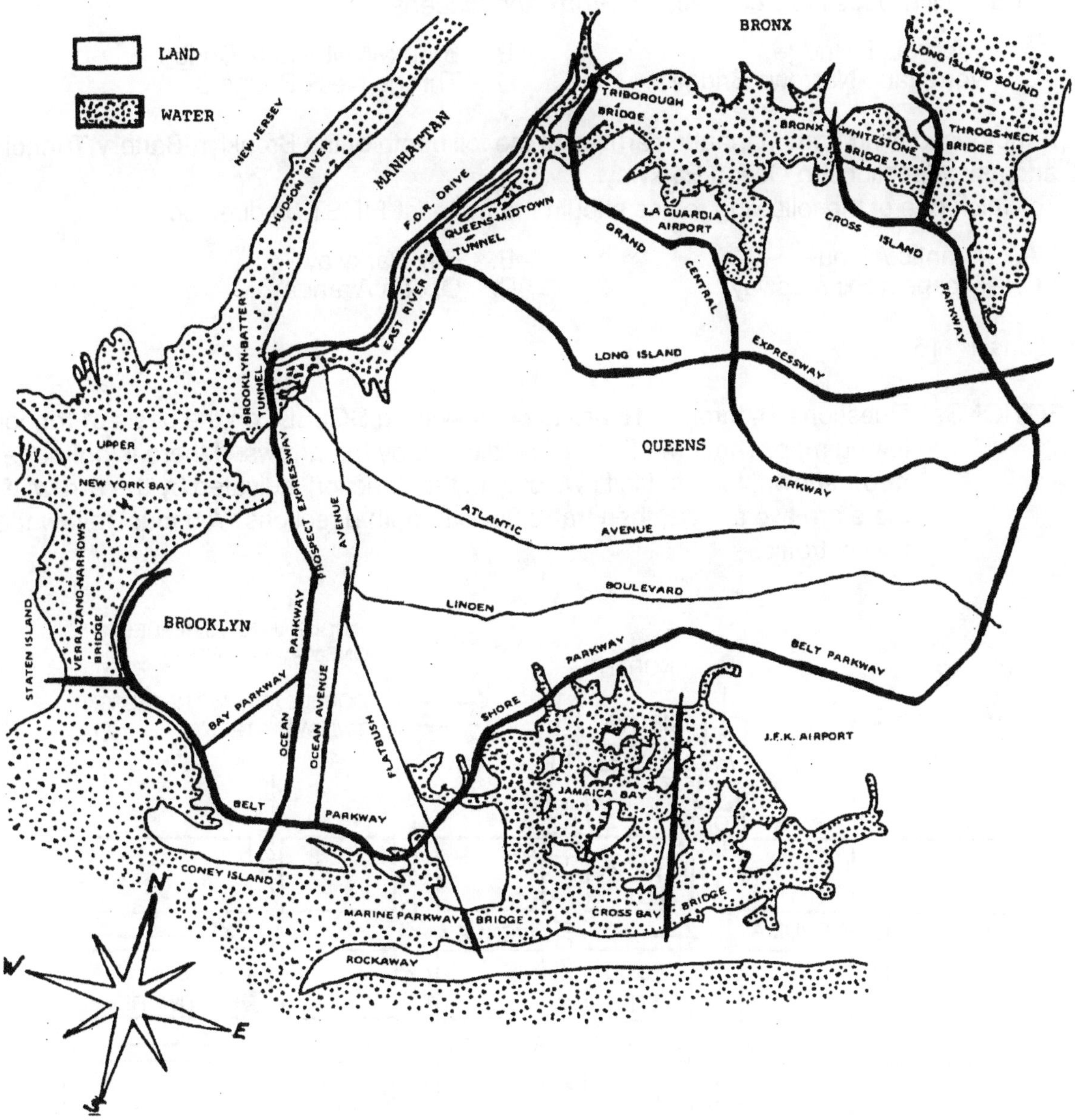

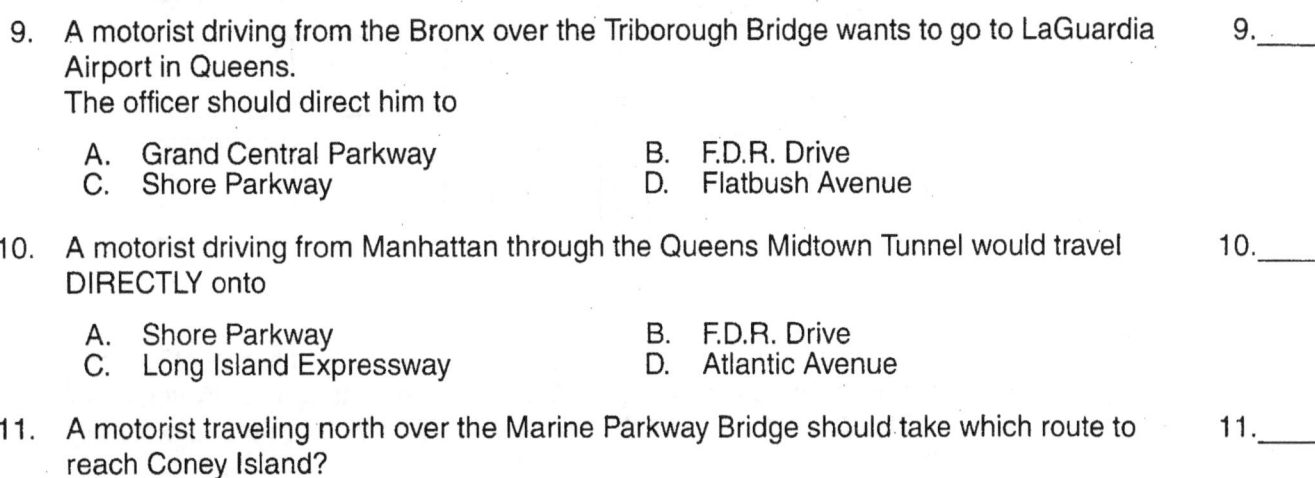

9. A motorist driving from the Bronx over the Triborough Bridge wants to go to LaGuardia Airport in Queens.
   The officer should direct him to

   A. Grand Central Parkway B. F.D.R. Drive
   C. Shore Parkway D. Flatbush Avenue

10. A motorist driving from Manhattan through the Queens Midtown Tunnel would travel DIRECTLY onto

    A. Shore Parkway B. F.D.R. Drive
    C. Long Island Expressway D. Atlantic Avenue

11. A motorist traveling north over the Marine Parkway Bridge should take which route to reach Coney Island?

    A. Shore Parkway East B. Belt Parkway West
    C. Linden Boulevard D. Ocean Parkway

12. Which facility does NOT connect the Bronx and Queens?　　12._____

    A. Triborough Bridge
    B. Bronx-Whitestone Bridge
    C. Verrazano-Narrows Bridge
    D. Throgs-Neck Bridge

13. A motorist driving from Manhattan arrives at the toll booth of the Brooklyn-Battery Tunnel　　13._____
    and asks directions to Ocean Parkway.
    To which one of the following routes should the motorist FIRST be directed?

    A. Atlantic Avenue
    B. Bay Parkway
    C. Prospect Expressway
    D. Ocean Avenue

Questions 14-16.

DIRECTIONS: Questions 14 through 16 are to be answered SOLELY on the basis of the following map. The flow of traffic is indicated by the arrows. If there is only one arrow shown, then traffic flows only in the direction indicated by the arrow. If there are two arrows, then traffic flows in both directions. You must follow the flow of traffic.

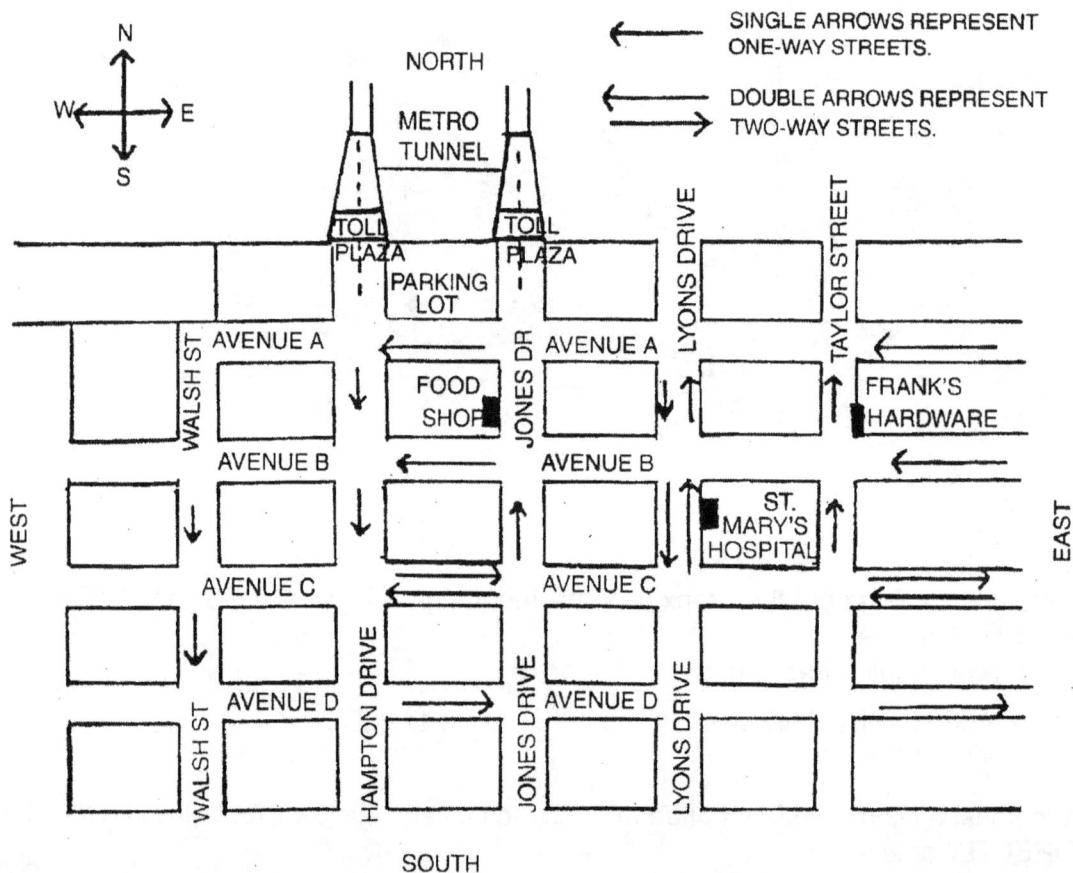

14. A motorist is exiting the Metro Tunnel and approaches the bridge and tunnel officer at the　　14._____
    toll plaza. He asks the officer how to get to the food shop on Jones Drive. Which one of the following is the SHORTEST route for the motorist to take, making sure to obey all traffic regulations?
    Travel south on Hampton Drive, then left on _____ on Jones Drive to the food shop.

A. Avenue A, then right
B. Avenue B, then right
C. Avenue D, then left
D. Avenue C, then left

15. A motorist heading south pulls up to a toll booth at the exit of the Metro Tunnel and asks Bridge and Tunnel Officer Evans how to get to Frank's Hardware Store on Taylor Street. Which one of the following is the SHORTEST route for the motorist to take, making sure to obey all traffic regulations?
Travel south on Hampton Drive, then east on

   A. Avenue B to Taylor Street
   B. Avenue D, then north on Taylor Street to Avenue B
   C. Avenue C, then north on Taylor Street to Avenue B
   D. Avenue C, then north on Lyons Drive, then east on Avenue B to Taylor Street

15.____

16. A motorist is exiting the Metro Tunnel and approaches the toll plaza. She asks Bridge and Tunnel Officer Owens for directions to St. Mary's Hospital. Which one of the following is the SHORTEST route for the motorist to take, making sure to obey all traffic regulations?
Travel south on Hampton Drive, then _____ on Lyons Drive to St. Mary's Hospital.

   A. left on Avenue D, then left
   B. right on Avenue A, then left on Walsh Street, then left on Avenue D, then left
   C. left on Avenue C, then left
   D. left on Avenue B, then right

16.____

Questions 17-18.

DIRECTIONS: Questions 17 and 18 are to be answered SOLELY on the basis of the map which appears on the following page. The flow of traffic is indicated by the arrows. If there is only one arrow shown, then traffic flows only in the direction indicated by the arrow. If there are two arrows shown, then traffic flows in both directions. You must follow the flow of traffic.

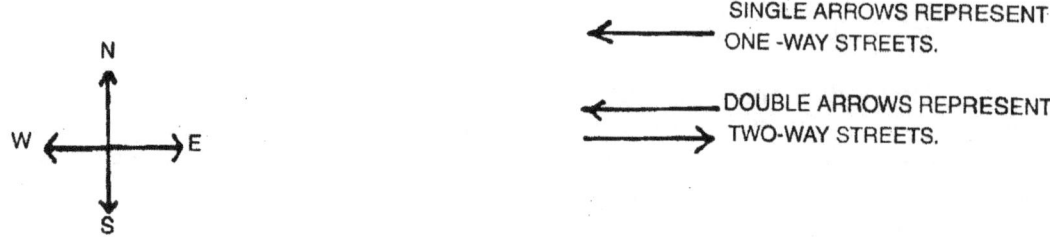

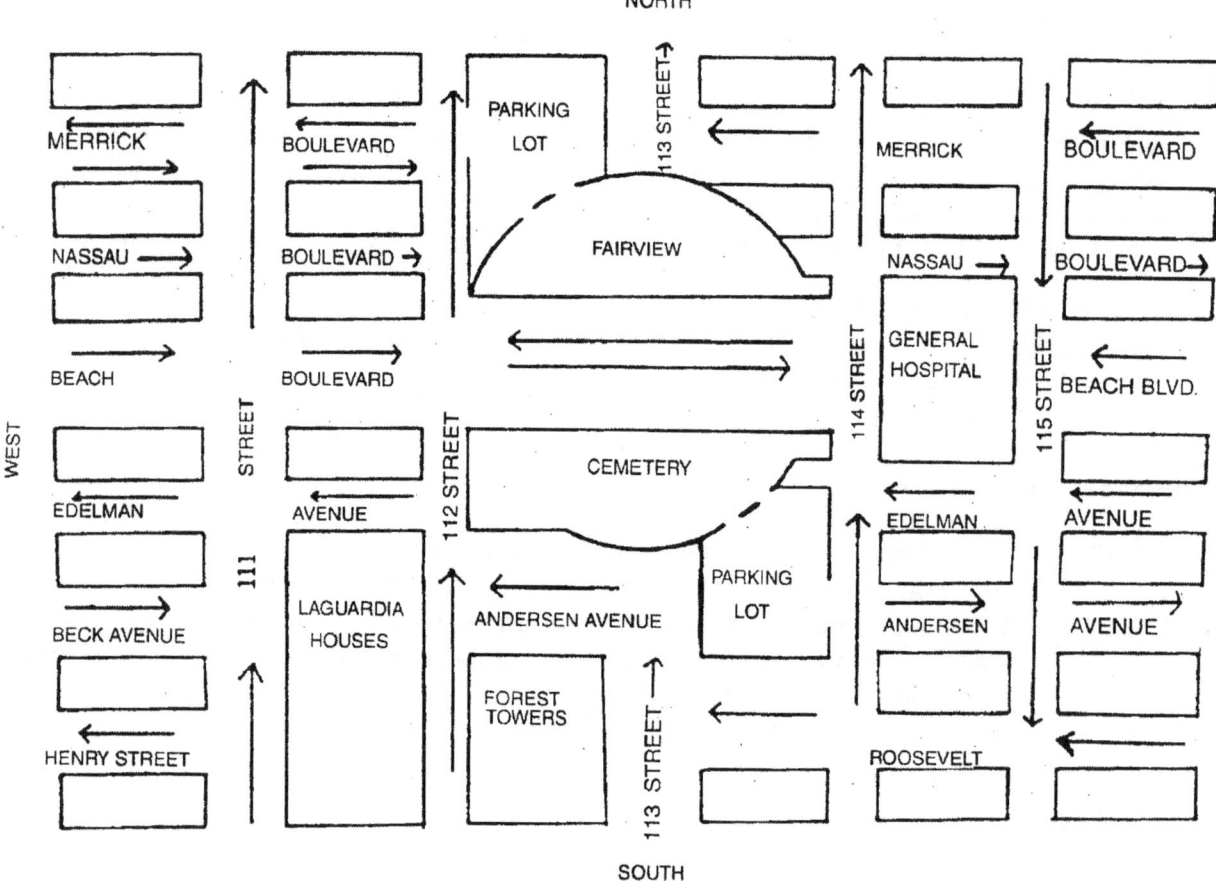

17. Police Officers Glenn and Albertson are on 111th Street at Henry Street when they are dispatched to a past robbery at Beach Boulevard and 115th Street.
Which one of the following is the SHORTEST route for the officers to follow in their patrol car, making sure to obey all traffic regulations?
Travel north on 111th Street, then east on _____ south on 115th Street.

 A. Edelman Avenue, then north on 112th Street, then east on Beach Boulevard, then north on 114th Street, then east on Nassau Boulevard, then one block
 B. Beach Boulevard, then north on 114th Street, then east on Nassau Boulevard, then one block
 C. Merrick Boulevard, then two blocks
 D. Nassau Boulevard, then south on 112th Street, then east on Beach Boulevard, then north on 114th Street, then east on Nassau Boulevard, then one block

18. Later in their tour, Officers Glenn and Albertson are driving on 114th Street. If they make a left turn to enter the parking lot at Andersen Avenue, and then make a u-turn, in what direction would they now be headed?

    A. North   B. South   C. East   D. West

Questions 19-20.

DIRECTIONS: Questions 19 and 20 are to be answered SOLELY on the basis of the following map. The flow of traffic is indicated by the arrows. If there is only one arrow shown, then traffic flows only in the direction indicated by the arrow. If there are two arrows shown, then traffic flows in both directions. You must follow the flow of traffic.

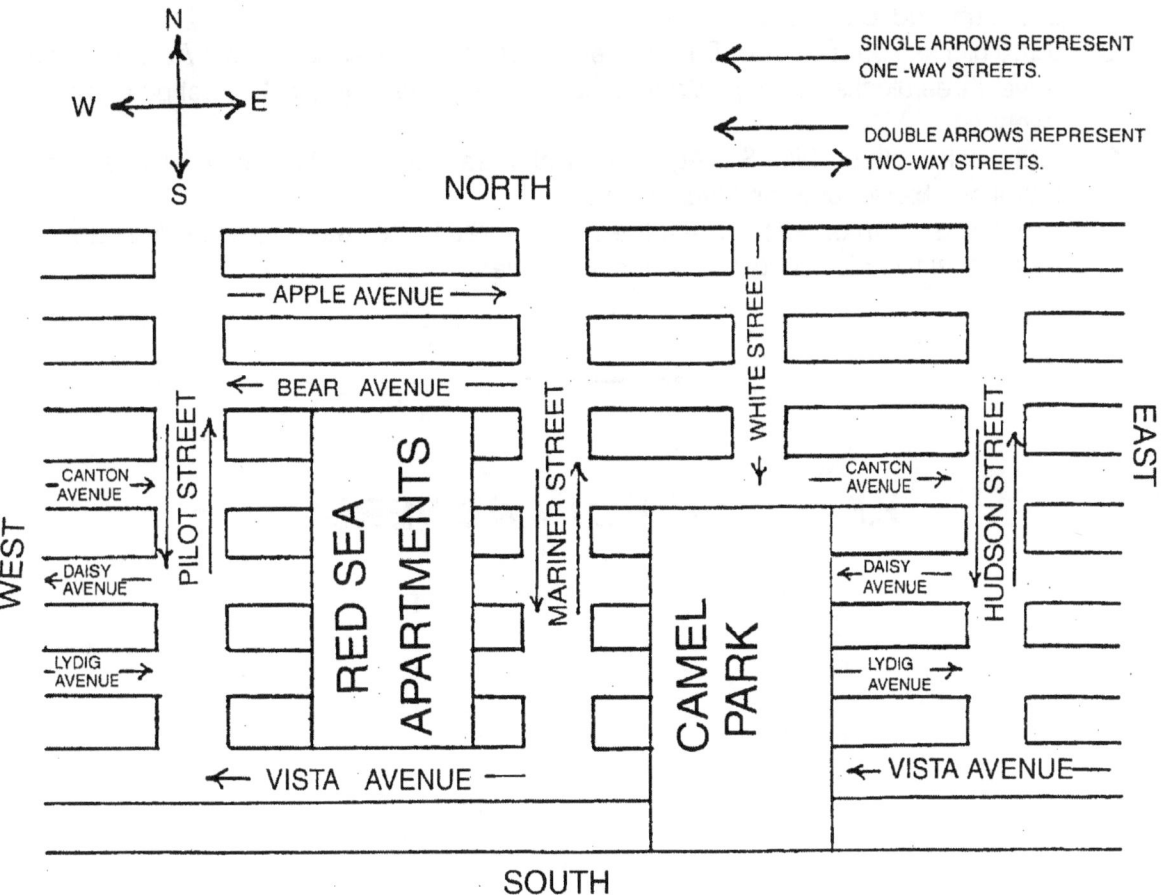

19. You are located at Apple Avenue and White Street. You receive a call to respond to the corner of Lydig Avenue and Pilot Street.
Which one of the following is the MOST direct route for you to take in your patrol car, making sure to obey all traffic regulations?
Travel _____ on Pilot Street.

    A. two blocks south on White Street, then one block east on Canton Avenue, then one block north on Hudson Street, then three blocks west on Bear Avenue, then three blocks south

    B. one block south on White Street, then two blocks west on Bear Avenue, then three blocks south

C. two blocks west on Apple Avenue, then four blocks south
D. two blocks south on White Street, then one block west on Canton Avenue, then three blocks south on Mariner Street, then one block west on Vista Avenue, then one block north

20. You are located at Canton Avenue and Pilot Street. You receive a call of a crime in progress at the intersection of Canton Avenue and Hudson Street.
Which one of the following is the MOST direct route for you to take in your patrol car, making sure to obey all traffic regulations?
Travel

   A. two blocks north on Pilot Street, then two blocks east on Apple Avenue, then one block south on White Street, then one block east on Bear Avenue, then one block south on Hudson Street
   B. three blocks south on Pilot Street, then travel one block east on Vista Avenue, then travel three blocks north on Mariner Street, then travel two blocks east on Canton Avenue
   C. one block north on Pilot Street, then travel three blocks east on Bear Avenue, then travel one block south on Hudson Street
   D. two blocks north on Pilot Street, then travel three blocks east on Apple Avenue, then travel two blocks south on Hudson Street

20. ____

KEY (CORRECT ANSWERS)

1. B
2. D
3. B
4. C
5. A
6. D
7. A
8. B
9. A
10. C
11. B/D
12. C
13. C
14. D
15. C
16. C
17. B
18. C
19. B
20. D